On Dreams

MAUREEN THORSON

BLOOF BOOKS

Published by Bloof Books
www.bloofbooks.com

Cover Art: Heather Goodwind, *Series 23 #17, The Bridge*, 2017, mixed media on canvas, 30 x 40 inches. Courtesy of Heather Goodwind.

ISBN-13: 978-1-7335294-3-3

1. Literary Collections—Essays. 2. Poetry—General. 3. Biography & Autobiography—Women. 4. Biography & Autobiography—Medical.

♾ This paper meets the requirements of ANSI/NISO Z39.48-1992

If a woman chances during her menstrual period to look into a highly polished mirror, the surface of it will grow cloudy with a blood-colored haze.

—Aristotle, *On Dreams*

Contents

Preface: On *On Dreams*

In DREAMS, cause and effect are tangled. Narrative is effaced. A mirror turns red because a woman looks at it.

People have long thought that dreams are prophetic. Mostly because they show us our fears.

It is best to confront one's fears directly—as in a mirror.

The rosy clouds float overhead, the sun is going down; and now the sandman's gentle tread comes stealing through the town.

How much of life is spent recounting the facts? How much of life is spent recounting what we think are the facts?

Hamlet tells the actors by whom he means to expose Claudius that their purpose "is to hold, as 'twere, the mirror up to nature."

At the time that Aristotle wrote his treatise *On Dreams*, the mirrors available in Greece were mainly made of polished metals like bronze and copper.

This might account for Aristotle's idea that a mirror could turn red. But it is more likely that Aristotle thought of a mirror as a sort of eye, a sense organ. Just as looking at a red object will create a green afterimage "in" my eye, so the mirror, by "looking" at a menstruating woman, takes on a red tinge.

Of course, Aristotle also wrote that men have more teeth than women. Without bothering to look in any mouths.

10   In a mirror, everything is transposed, left, right; right, left. You see yourself, but not as others see you.

The statements I make—how can anyone be sure that they're true? Not that I mean to lie but, like Aristotle, I may have my blind spots, my misconceptions. My vanities.

Narcissus nodding into his own reflection.

For example, it has been my dream to seem authoritative, like Aristotle, if nothing else. After all, who wouldn't want to appear objective? Wouldn't at least pretend to it?

Answer: persons with a better relationship to reality than myself.

15   The poet Doug Lang once wrote a series of reminiscences, each concluding with the sentence, "I knew it was a dream because . . . everything is."

Row, row, row your boat . . .

My relationship to truth may be dreamlike at best. I must admit to subtle differences in the same memory, recalled now, recalled again.

In an essay on movies in which women, or more often young girls, become possessed, Danielle Pafunda quotes the ancient Greek physician Aretaeus of Cappadocia: "In women, in the hollow of the body below the ribcage, lies the womb. It is very much like an independent animal within the body, for it moves around of its own accord and is quite erratic."

And if I said, there is some truth to that, would a mirror flush at the sight of me?

Dickinson's admonition that we "tell all the truth, but tell it slant" presupposes that we know what truth is. But if we only intuit it, "as in a glass, darkly"?

20

"Human kind cannot bear very much reality," wrote T. S. Eliot. Hence poetry? Hence the remove of a mirror?

[THIS PAGE INTENTIONALLY LEFT BLANK]

Left, right. Right, left.

The Woman, the Mirror, the Eye

Our senses are imperfect: our ears deceive us, our eyes play tricks. So we need other means by which to triangulate reality.

Mirrors might be one. They show us things that our eyes can't see. Principally ourselves.

But mirrors are imperfect, too. As I've read so often, the objects in them may be closer than they appear.

Dreams are another possible source of insight. But the world is what we agree on. And how can we agree on a dream?

"All men whilst they are awake are in one common world; but . . . each of them, when he is asleep, is in a world of his own," wrote Plutarch. And so, to quote the Scottish physician Robert Macnish, "there is a strong analogy between dreaming and insanity." 5

After a sudden onset of fuzzy, doubled vision, I was told that I might be losing my sight. It could take years for the process to complete itself. Or perhaps it would not. But already, the doctor told me, large blind spots had taken root in my right eye.

In *Through the Looking-Glass*, Tweedledee and Tweedledum inform Alice that they are all part of a dream that the sleeping Red King is having, and that when he wakes, they'll "go out—bang!—just like a candle!"

Shortly after learning of my blind spots, I came across an article about mirrors in folklore. It described a Chinese legend that says our reflections are separate beings, condemned to sleepwalk through life, dumbly mimicking our actions.

Several years before the blind spots were diagnosed, I experienced bright blue flashes occluding my vision. I was referred to a neurologist. But when I went to see him, the neurologist was angry. He thought I was wasting his time. In his opinion, I was "seeing things."

10 Yes, of course. That was why I was there. But he meant that I was crazy. That I was failing to live in our common reality.

Whose reality?

In her essay "Finding Poetry in Illness," Jennifer Nix writes: "Those who haven't suffered serious illness rarely understand how isolating it can be."

In describing menstruating women's effect on mirrors, Aristotle posits a scene that is part of no common reality I've experienced. A scene that could only happen in a dream.

Still, does that make it insane to believe that a woman's cycle will color a mirror? Aristotle was wrong, but was he crazy?

Back to the Chinese legend. It says that our reflections will someday throw off their torpor and attack us. The flickering movements we catch in mirrors, out of the corners of our eyes, are their first stirrings.   15

Between the blue flashes and the blind spots, I have been tested four times for colorblindness. As if I would not notice.

Would I notice?

In *Ways of Seeing*, John Berger describes the Western tradition of painting naked women so as to gratify the viewer's desire, while hypocritically shaming the women for their nudity.

There is also a feeling of unasked-for shame in being seen as sick, although one feels like a locus of repulsion or pity, rather than desire. But in both cases, the person beheld is not really seen as a person, but as an object, a lesson. In both cases, the beheld represents a moral error.

Even so, I could look into a mirror for hours.   20

The Chinese legend interests me enough to conduct further research. But I find that there is no such legend at all. Instead, the whole idea seems to trace—of course—to Borges.

For hours—were it not that I have bad dreams.

In the wake of my diagnosis, I felt cut off from others. Did being labeled as sick create the distance, or did it make me conscious of a gap that was always there?

Writing is a vain, heartbreaking, and lonely act, like waving at oneself in a mirror.

25 A few weeks after my diagnosis, when I could no longer stand the radically different images produced by my afflicted eyes, I taped the worst of them shut, and went around one-eyed for a day. Without depth perception, it was as though I were walking (and sometimes tripping) through a painting.

All hail the vanishing point.

Brunelleschi is said to have discovered linear perspective with the aid of a mirror.

Linear perspective makes paintings seem more "real"—that is to say, less like the flat rectangles that they actually are.

In Hans Holbein the Younger's painting *The Ambassadors*, there is a curious, elongated object at the foot of the table on which the portrait's subjects lean. Only when the painting is viewed from an angle does the object take on its correct proportions, revealing itself as a human skull.

Biologists assess the mental acuity of animals by testing whether they can recognize themselves in mirrors. Very few animals pass the mirror test: the great apes, elephants, dolphins and killer whales, magpies. 30

Humans pass the test only from the age of eighteen months onward.

There is just one surviving nude by Diego Velázquez, the court painter to Spain's Philip IV. It depicts Venus in the style pioneered by Titian: stretched out on a couch, her reflection visible in a mirror that Cupid holds before her.

The mirror test strikes me as flawed in that it treats vanity as a sign of intelligence.

After all, certain animals—pigs, for example—can determine that there is food behind them by seeing it reflected in a mirror, but take no interest in their own reflections.

It is usually said that Velázquez's Venus is admiring herself. But the viewer can see Venus's reflection in the mirror that Cupid holds in front of her. This would seem to mean that Venus is not using the mirror to look at herself: she is using it to look at you. 35

Velázquez's most famous painting also employs a mirror. *Las Meninas* depicts a princess of Spain with her ladies in waiting, two dwarfs, a dog, Velázquez himself before a canvas, and a distant courtier upon a stair. Then, small, dark, but nearly in the center of the painting, the reflections of the King and Queen of Spain, ostensibly the subjects of the painted painter's work, posed just where the viewer stands, looking in and over the scene.

Velázquez's *Venus* has long been in the collection of England's National Gallery. In 1914, it was severely damaged when the canvas was slashed through by a knife-wielding suffragette.

The narrative that subsequently developed in the press was more suited to attempted murder than vandalism, treating the painted image as though it were flesh and blood, and the woman who had "injured" it as two-dimensional, a slavering maniac.

The perspective we see in paintings is, of course, false. There is no depth within the canvas. All representative painting may be said, in this way, to "trompe l'oeil," that is, to fool the eye.

40 Neurologists have discovered a system of "mirror neurons" in the human brain, which fire when a person performs an action and also when a person sees another perform it.

Some neurologists argue that mirror neurons explain the human ability to learn through mimicry and to anticipate other people's motivations. Others think these neurologists are seeing what they want to see, and extrapolating wildly from what is only partly understood.

"We are for flat forms because they destroy illusion and reveal truth," wrote Alfred Gottlieb and Mark Rothko. Or Magritte, more playfully, "Ceci n'est pas une pipe."

There is an ancient Greek story about two painters, Zeuxis and Parrhasius. They compete to see who can make the most realistic painting. Zeuxis paints grapes so lusciously that birds fly down to eat them. Parrhasius, in turn, invites Zeuxis to pull back the curtains drawn over his painting. But the curtains themselves are the painting—and Parrhasius wins.

In one of his 1964 seminars on psychoanalysis, Lacan makes use of this story to describe an aspect of the human mind that separates us from animals. It is our love of trompe l'oeil in the sense of Parrhasius's painted curtain: an urge toward what is hidden.

In an essay on Shakespeare's *Venus and Adonis*, Catherine   45
Belsey glosses Lacan's concept of trompe l'oeil as "the promise of a presence that it fails to deliver."

Writing, like painting, attempts to make a clear picture cohere from the mess of experience. It promises to deliver—and fails.

"The truth is more important than the facts," wrote Frank Lloyd Wright.

Hamlet thought that art's purpose was to hold a mirror up to life. Oscar Wilde said it was to conceal anything but beauty. But what do we get out of all this mirroring and concealing? A simulacrum? Lacan's irresistibly ersatz semblant?

The condition I was diagnosed with is called acute zonal occult outer retinopathy (AZOOR). Its primary characteristic is that it can't be seen.

50 At least, not directly. An AZOOR sufferer's retina appears perfectly healthy—no dead spots or occlusions. AZOOR can only be inferred by testing the patient's field of vision, one eye at a time, mapping the large blind spots that characterize the condition like someone sounding a bay.

You look at the eye—AZOOR's not there. You look at what the eye sees—ah, there it is.

After receiving my diagnosis, I went back to my job as a lawyer, where I pored over long, tiny-fonted legal documents for hours, growing angrier and angrier, wondering if they might be the last thing I see.

How do you tell the truth about an illness so rare there's virtually nothing written about it? A diagnosis that is itself uncertain, because the disease's primary symptom is that nothing appears physically wrong?

After being told I could be going blind, I became angry. Soon, I was angry all the time. But no one seemed to notice. I began to feel as if I were going crazy, as if the only way anyone would *get it* were if I had some kind of sordid breakdown.

Instead, I wrote poems. 55

In "Tradition and the Individual Talent," T. S. Eliot wrote that "poetry is not a turning loose of emotion, but an escape from emotion; it is not the expression of personality, but an escape from personality."

Yes, and mirrors turn red when menstruating women look at them.

Still, I'd like to be free from emotion, though I suspect that a person who expresses none is far less sane than one who expresses too much.

The psychiatrist Anna Fels speculates that writers are better proofed against tragedy than other people. Whether crossed by a perfidious lover or a frail body, the writer can wrest back the narrative, retell and shape it, and, finally, call it her own.

Hello, book. Hello, little mirror of my suffering. 60

The "ill-formed offspring of my feeble brain," as Anne Bradstreet said. More Caliban than Ariel?

The blind poet is a romantic notion. We ascribe a clairvoyance, literally a kind of "clear seeing," to Homer and Milton. But the only insight I've received from my eye problems is into the fitfulness of our illusions of control.

And even as I write this, I question my right to do so. I haven't suffered very greatly.

Of course, as Zora Neale Hurston warned, "if you are silent about your pain, they'll kill you and say you enjoyed it."

65   Anyway, silence can't protect you from emotion, from personality.

So here I am, telling you all this, exposing my vulnerability, my rawness and doubt, and feeling ashamed of myself for telling. Even now, per John Berger, I connive in treating myself as a sight.

Of course, I *am* a sight. A writer writes to be read.

If silence can't save you from emotion, writing can't save you from going blind. But writing offers the reductive simplicity of narrative, with its seductive endings, tidy resolutions.

It offers a simulacrum of control, an opportunity to appear acceptably placed within the confines of our common reality.

70   No one asked T. S. Eliot whether he *deserved* to escape. It was enough that he could.

And I can try, at least for a while. The unreality of words, hiding in plain sight their lack of three dimensions, is no worse than any other.

What a strange dream!, the Red King thought, waking with a start.

Meet Aristotle

I HAVE BEEN TRYING to tell myself a story about Aristotle. The story seeks to explain a statement that seems to reflect a shocking credulity, intellectual laziness, or both.

"Narrative is a process whose function is knowing," observes Jordan Davis, echoing William James.

Not much is known about Aristotle's life. Sources describe even his death only vaguely, as due to "a disease of the stomach," or, more quaintly, "a digestive complaint."

Oscar Wilde wrote that art should reveal only itself and not the artist. Aristotle left many ideas behind, but no biography, no sense of self. Does this mean that Aristotle was an artist?

Being an artist requires not just self-effacement, but self-deception. To quote Philip Roth on writing fiction: "The idea is to perceive your invention as a reality that can be understood as a dream." 5

In his 1974 commencement address at Caltech, Richard Feynman recounted the cautionary tale of the first scientist to measure the charge of an electron. The scientist measured it incorrectly, but was held in such high esteem that, for many years, other scientists who got different answers figured that they, instead, must be the ones measuring incorrectly.

While researching Aristotle's death, I discover his treatise *On the Parts of Animals*. Here, Aristotle claims that male and female animals have different types of stomachs. One commentator describes this claim as "strange," and without "anatomical foundation." Another demurs, stating that, "without knowing the animal models that Aristotle was using, I am not prepared to be so bold."

Stanford University's *Encyclopedia of Philosophy* provides some biographical information on Aristotle, but cautions that in the absence of contemporaneous accounts, much of it is "speculative." As a result, the *Encyclopedia* laments, "sometimes thinly attested conclusions gain credence only by dint of repetition."

Personally, I stand ready to gain credence by dint of repetition. It seems to have worked for Aristotle.

10   After all, in the two-plus millennia since his death, no one has discovered a species with stomachs corresponding to Aristotle's description. Yet we are "not prepared to be so bold" as to discount his statements.

Aristotle is regarded as one of the fathers of science. But this is because he espoused inductive reasoning, not because he developed or applied any principles or methods we would today consider "scientific."

In harping on Aristotle's biography, am I trying to turn him into flesh and blood? Am I trying to invent him? To invent myself?

One of the attractions and difficulties of inductive reasoning: it implicitly allows that the premises, and therefore the conclusions, may be incorrect.

Regarding Aristotle's personality, Stanford notes that some sources describe him as "snide and arrogant," while others paint him as friendly, open, and "tirelessly interested in expanding the frontiers of human knowledge."

What really killed Aristotle? Was it stomach cancer? An ulcer? A bad olive?

I begin to feel a little sorry for Aristotle. Did he like oranges? It is not "important" to know whether Aristotle liked oranges. But when we think about people we've lost, people we've loved, we think about things like that.

Did someone think of dead Aristotle, think, "I loved how he always whistled between his teeth?"

15

Arthur Schopenhauer noted that for every memory we retain, a thousand are forgotten. We recall the events of our own lives only marginally better than those of a novel we've read.

And with nothing to work from, we don't remember Aristotle's life at all.

20   It doesn't do, of course, for me to feel sorry for Aristotle. He is my symbol, a cipher. I other him, I define myself in contrast.

And rereading his blithe and ridiculous statement regarding mirrors, women, and menstruation, I can content myself that he started it.

In her essay "Narrative/Identity," kari edwards observes that while narrative underpins identity, identity is constantly shifting. And so, she asks, "doesn't that sort of put the super-ego on a permanent holiday?"

"Reality is merely an illusion, albeit a very persistent one," wrote Albert Einstein. And Feynman again: "The first principle is that you must not fool yourself—and you are the easiest person to fool."

If I can pity Aristotle, it is because I have found a way to make him small and uncertain. A man and not a monolith.

25   I lied, of course, in saying I've been trying to tell a story about Aristotle. I've been trying to tell a story about myself. Like all stories, it needed an antagonist.

But that's not true either. In trying to stop fooling myself long enough to perceive the world clearly, I don't need Aristotle as an antagonist.

Still, here I am, shadowboxing a 2300-year-old dead guy. This says more about me than him. Clearly, I'm no artist.

In the dream, I'm riding the subway when Aristotle enters the car and sits next to me. His toga's pockets bulge with note-books and a bottle of Maalox. This is my chance—I could ask where he heard about women and mirrors, ask him anything, really. But I persist in my ignorance, staring distantly ahead.

A Good Attitude

A CLOSE RELATIVE of mine, upon getting her first period, declared that she wouldn't put up with it.

In his essay "Against Conceptualism," Cal Bedient asserts that control is the primary concern of the Oulipo and other "method poetries." For adherents of these schools, "emotion is volatile and unpredictable, whereas method is safe and reliable."

Menstruation has never seemed terribly important to me, even as it has functioned as an overt marker of my femininity. As when a doctor asked my mother, at one of my routine checkups, "Is she a señorita yet?"

I wasn't. Later, of course, I went from chica to señorita overnight.

The classicist Rosamond Kent Sprague notes that Aristotle's 5 claim regarding women's effect on mirrors "was for a considerable time regarded as too indelicate for the English reader," with the result that British translators simply left it in the original Greek.

I once read an essay by a woman who valued her cycle. She went off the pill and wished she'd done so years earlier. Each day now had its particular flavor, its harmonic resonance, reverence.

I can't say I've ever found menstruation transcendent, but maybe it could be. I enjoy seasons—planting and harvest, watching the moon. Perhaps I could be my own seasons and moon?

It sounds lovely, although unlikely. Lovely *because* unlikely?

In his essay "A Fine Excess," James Longenbach warns that "restraint may seem merely banal, an unexamined trust of limitation." At the same time, "excess may seem obvious, an unexamined romance with transgression—except inasmuch as a particular work of art creates the context in which a particular aesthetic choice becomes a virtue."

10 What are the manly virtues? The womanly virtues? The humanly virtues?

I'm not really sure what I can achieve by telling you about menstruation. Maybe, like Kate Zambreno, I am "resist[ing] the urge to write down only the manageable."

Here is a possible insight into why so many men take midlife hard—seem so suddenly to hear "Time's wingéd chariot." They've been used to a certain roboticness of the body, a clean machine. Whereas, from the age of twelve or thirteen, most women have been rather regularly reminded that they are flesh and blood.

Or were. The birth control pill operates such that women can skip their periods. But the pill was originally (and then for decades) marketed only in a formulation that included a week of placebo pills, allowing for a pseudo-period to occur. The drug companies worried that without this induced period, women would reject the pill as unnatural.

I have to wonder if any women were consulted in this decision.

We can manipulate the body, but the body remains. So why not use others' fear of it against them? If only for a laugh.

In high school, for example, my best friend and I snuck a dozen donuts into the movies by stuffing the box into the bottom of a backpack and throwing dozens of maxi pads on top. The poor kid manning (boying?) the theater, upon gazing into the backpack, which we'd unzipped at his insistence, didn't know which way to look. He waved us and our secret donuts through, with a harrowed expression on his pale and pimply face.

In the short story "Rich Girls Will Break Your Heart," Craig Foltz questions: "How to practice restraint without exposing it as something artificial?"

Why mind the artificiality? We spend our lives trying to erect barriers around our frailty, to logic and bluster in the face of the world's uncontrollable indifference. And the end is always the same.

"I'm not putting up with this."

20   Artificiality is how you know it's human. Excessiveness is how you know it too.

Do you remember the old *The Kids in the Hall* sketch, the one in which a grinning Dave Foley declares that he has a good attitude toward menstruation?

I am trying to develop a good attitude toward a total lack of control.

Confessions of a Pareidoliac

OUR ANCESTORS survived in great part due to their ability to group things, to categorize and see patterns.

This ability is so ingrained that we see patterns where there are none—faces in the bark of trees, purpose in random chance, a "woman" where really there is me.

There is a word for this: *pareidolia*. It's a phenomenon that artists have long found useful.

The sixteenth-century painter Giuseppe Arcimboldo developed a humorous pareidoliac specialty—grotesque portraits that, upon further study, reveal themselves not as human faces, but agglomerations of books, vegetables, flowers, and fish.

As Arcimboldo's work implies, our predilection for finding patterns can lead us into error. Sometimes that slender, curling silhouette waving about in a tree really is a snake. And sometimes it's not.

Stephanie Burt puts it this way: "the assumption of likeness is always a fiction."

In 1927, Constantin Brancusi attempted to bring a sculpture, *Bird in Space*, into the United States for an exhibition organized by Marcel Duchamp. Brancusi presented the sculpture to Customs officials as a duty-free work of art. The officials disagreed, reclassifying it as a dutiable "manufacture of metal." Brancusi challenged the decision in court.

Truth is stranger than fiction.

In the *Odyssey*, Penelope explains why dreams seem to be either pointless or prophetic, punning on the similarity in ancient Greek of the words for *horn* and *truth*, and the words for *ivory* and *deceit*: "For two are the gates of shadowy dreams, and one is fashioned of horn and one of ivory. Those dreams that pass through the gate of sawn ivory deceive men, bringing words that find no fulfillment. But those that come forth through the gate of polished horn bring true things to pass, when any mortal sees them."

10   I once purchased a book of interviews exploring how dreams influence writers' work. Despite the glowing, new-agey promises of the back cover, many interviewees struggled to connect their writing with their dreams. Others seemed suspicious of the whole idea.

I don't blame them. After all, if one were to admit that one's creative work was drawn directly from dreams, from the unconscious, that unordered messy nothing, then how could one claim genius in the result? How could a dream be art?

As an irritable Mark Strand put it in a 1998 interview in the *Paris Review*, "People who write down their dreams and think they're poems are wrong. They're neither dreams nor poems."

One of my college professors argued that the lack of perspective in the icons of Andrei Rublev was intentional, meant to reinforce the idea that the divine realm being depicted—which for Rublev was the true world—isn't like this one at all.

In other words, Rublev's icons are neither dreams nor paintings. They're real.

The sociobiologist Robert Trivers notes that, when people feel as though they are not in control of their lives, their patternmaking impulses go into overdrive, leading them to see elaborate correspondences in random data.

In his treatise *On Dreams*, Aristotle argues that dreams are the detritus of the past day's events, remixed and toyed with by the sleeping mind. By contrast, in his later work of the same name, the early Christian bishop Synesius of Cyrene writes that dreams provide rich and poor alike with divine insight.

Because each dreamer is unique, Synesius advises that there can be no standardized dream interpretations; one might as well assume that all mirrors reflect the same object. Instead, he counsels readers to record their dreams, the better to track how they manifest themselves in the waking world.

"Nobody fact-checks dreams, of course," writes Christopher Benley.

Contemporary explanations of dreaming mostly follow the dichotomy sketched by Aristotle and Synesius. Either they're just a meaningless byproduct of the brain's assimilation of information into memory, as Aristotle and neurologists would have it, or they provide insight into fundamental realities, per Synesius and psychoanalysts.

20 Of course, there's at least one important distinction between Freud and Synesius. Synesius thought your dreams predicted your future; Freud thought they revealed your past.

Regardless, maybe it's not the truth of the pattern that matters, but the belief in it.

Plato threw poets out of his Republic because he saw them as mere imitators of the world, instead of, like philosophers, its interrogators.

But neither poets nor philosophers stand beyond the world. They are in the world, and part of it.

I find it hard not to blame people for what they do in my dreams. When I dream that someone is treating me badly, I figure my subconscious is trying to tell me something.

25 As Aristotle put it, "the soul makes assertions in sleep."

One commonly remarked-on feature of dreams is that we don't notice their senselessness until we're awake.

But I'm not sure why we would expect dreams to make sense, when our waking lives so often fail to observe narrative convention.

The truth is, our lives aren't stories. In stories, things happen for a reason.

When I was a kid, I enjoyed swinging the mirrored door of the bathroom medicine cabinet toward the larger mirror on the wall, and sticking my hand in between. So many hands, all waving!

At least, I enjoyed it until some girl at school told me how 30 Bloody Mary could appear in any mirror, so long as you called for her. After that, I spent about six months afraid to look into mirrors at all.

Bloody Mary aside, the act of staring fixedly into mirrors often produces hallucinations, due to what's called the Troxler Effect.

It works like this: When you stare at a single point, your brain quickly ceases to process anything on the extreme periphery. Instead, it replaces those details with a cobbled-together image of the thing you're staring at.

So if you stare deeply into a mirror, you may see garbled replicas of your own face floating on the edge of sight.

The poet Jessica Smith has noted the commonalities between astrological writing and certain avant-garde writing. A system is presumed to exist, and the work extrapolates from it.

35   But what kind of system?

Oxford professor Deborah Cameron has devoted her career to combating the notion that men and women use language differently. She explains that ideas like this are dangerous precisely because, "whether or not they are 'true' in any historical or scientific sense, [they] have consequences in the real world. They shape our beliefs, and so influence our actions."

Among all my acquaintances, it is my women friends that seem most interested in alternatives to formal logic—divination, astrology, tarot, dream interpretation.

One could read this as a form of illusory pattern recognition. Feeling themselves shut out from the traditional pathways of control, they adopt other methods of making meaning.

"Storylessness, after all, has been women's big problem," writes Katha Politt.

40   But why should women adopt an alternative to logical reasoning, when doing so may expose them to criticisms—of

flightiness, unseriousness, unintelligence—that presumably they hope to avoid?

Here's a thought: once someone extrapolating from false premises has built up the case for your not actually being human, you might be tempted to chuck the whole concept of logic as flawed.

Or maybe it's just fun to troll the self-appointed logicians by calling yourself a witch.

When you know how others see the world, you can manipulate them. I concede that one of the reasons I became a lawyer is that when someone hears that you are one, they perceive you as *dangerous*.

But regardless of whether my silhouette, waving about in the tree, is like that of a snake or a lawyer or a woman (or possibly all three), only one thing seems really certain. I'm me.

According to Aristotle, the red flush left by a menstruating woman's gaze is difficult to remove from a new mirror, but quite simple to remove from an old one.   45

Fool me once, shame on you. Fool me twice . . .

I like the idea that getting older renders me less susceptible to error. But it could be that age simply hardens one's distortions.

Sylvia Plath's poem "Mirror" sinisterly recounts, from a mirror's point of view, what is said to be a common experience for the aging—that of being continuously surprised that one's reflection does not remain the same as it was, say, at seventeen.

I didn't very much like being a child. I wanted to grow up. Not so that I could have a boyfriend or a car or eat ice cream for dinner. I wanted self-assuredness. Grown-ups, I thought, knew what they were doing.

50 After twenty-odd years as a grown-up, all I can say is, well, there goes another unfounded belief.

Feng shui teaches that it is unlucky to have a mirror facing your bed. I've had a mirror facing my bed for the past eight years, and there it will stay. I mean, at some point, you have to stop believing everything you hear.

Or see.

Plath's poem inscribes the same horror as the Bloody Mary story: that of looking into a mirror and seeing something other than what you think you ought.

But what we see in mirrors is already wrong, transposing left and right.

55 Here's an old brainteaser for you: if left and right are transposed in mirrors, why aren't up and down?

The answer is that mirrors don't transpose left and right at all. We consider reflections transposed only because left and right are contextual. Your right, my left.

Artists besides Arcimboldo have benefited from the eccentricities of human vision. For example, many observers perceive the flowers in Monet's painting "Poppies at Argenteuil" as actually shaking, blown by a wind that isn't there.

The illusion is produced by Monet's use of paints of different colors, but equal reflectiveness. We normally rely on the relative brightness of objects to judge their positions. When everything is equally bright, our brains can't decide which things are in front and which are behind. And so we see them as glittering, subtly shifting in space.

Is a painting that pulses with such indeterminacy more accurate in its representation of the world? Or less?

Regardless, the painting is part of the world that it purports   60
to represent.

At the time that Brancusi sued the Customs Service, objects were considered "art" for legal purposes only if they closely and accurately imitated nature. A journalist reporting on Brancusi's lawsuit scoffed that, under this test, the greatest sculpture of all time would be a podiatrist's model of a bunion-afflicted foot.

In the short reflection "Borges and I," Borges describes how he resists transforming completely from his shy, private self into the loud and boisterous public Borges, who fame constantly threatens to make more real.

The final sentence professes uncertainty as to which Borges is writing the page.

Asking me how I feel is like asking which way the wind is blowing. Right now the wind may be in the north—but in a day, an hour, a minute—the wind will blow another way.

65 Maybe if I wrote twelve different versions of every event on clear plastic sheets and then stapled them on top of each other I'd approximate lived experience.

Instead, I create and present the Maureen on this page. A person you can never speak with, never answer, or take to task. Nor can I.

She exists inviolate here. And here she stays. As I move on and away from her, as we find ourselves farther and farther apart.

Rosalie Moore wrote that "the mind's disguise is permanence." In other words, constancy of self is just a pattern that we perceive.

In *The Situation and the Story*, Vivian Gornick explains the distinction between the writer and her on-page persona this way: the persona is "apparently, only her solid, limited self—and she [is] in control."

A writer, by contrast, is a real person, and thus in control of nothing—though she can try to manipulate the way you perceive her.   70

To quote Borges again, "the original is unfaithful to the translation."

I'm an emotional mess in real life. But here, on the page, I am calm, collected, distilled into perfection.

But wait—am I an emotional mess in real life? I might feel like one, but people are always telling me how controlled I seem.

The face begins to fit the mask. The writer is part of the world.

And still our perception of the external is complicated by our   75
interiority, by the things of which, according to Yeats, "Man makes a superhuman / Mirror-resembling dream."

There's the I that I see, the I that I want others to see, and the I that they actually see.

With such complications, perceiving the world clearly requires both fine-tuned faith in, and deep skepticism about, one's judgment.

In an essay on John Berryman's *Dream Songs*, Robert Lowell describes the poems as not dreams but "a waking hallucination."

In other words, the dreams aren't dreams. They're life.

80   At the end of the *Bird in Space* trial, the court found for Brancusi, holding that his sculpture reflected a "so-called new school of art, whose exponents attempt to portray abstract ideas rather than to imitate natural objects."

Because he saw the world as subject to an overarching order, Synesius faulted Penelope for believing that any dreams were false. Rather, he argued, the dreamer had simply not yet penetrated their meaning.

If truth is stranger than fiction, then the art that most accurately mimics reality would be as strange as possible. Dreamlike. A pattern extrapolated from the assumption of, rather than the reality of, a system.

Unlike Synesius, I don't believe that the world is subject to an overarching order. But I'm sympathetic to his claim that if a person were "placed outside of the world, he could not any longer use his knowledge; because he exercises it upon the world, and by means of the world."

Imagine trying to find your way with a compass that *wants* every direction to be north.

This is more or less where we are, perceiving the world around 85 us by means of instruments that find patterns everywhere.

We're in it, and of it. Really living the dream.

And so, in the words of Judge Waite of the United States Customs Court, "let judgment be entered accordingly."

Double-Paned

SOME SAY THE EYES are the windows of the soul; others say they are the soul's mirror.

The truth is they're both: while I regard my reflection in your eye's convex surface, you see me through it.

Jean Cocteau once admonished mirrors to "reflect a little more before sending back images." Good advice for eyeballs, too.

I spend time lurking in a Facebook discussion about an article featuring young women poets accompanied by overtly sexual photographs. The discussion turns to the arbitrary dividing line between the youthful-and-hot and the not-so-youthful, and how this line implicates experience versus naivete.

Soon, the conversants are talking about Medusa.

5

I imagine Medusa's mom catching her posting selfies, giving duck face, trying hard not to turn the screen into stone.

The notion that the act of seeing can alter the thing seen would seem to be confirmed, if on a tiny scale, by quantum physics.

Of course, the inverse is also true. Seeing alters the seer.

In her introduction to *The Poethical Wager*, Joan Retallack writes that "the image of horizon that has been so crucial to romantic idealist philosophies and literatures may not be a threshold of possibility at all, unless one locates possibility in a mirror."

10   Instead, Retallack advocates "radical unknowability [as] the only constant." When her alter ego, Quinta Slef, calls that "a daunting view if part of your program is ethical or political," Retallack retorts that "it's daunting if your primary concern is control."

Well, and if it is?

The word *panopticon* comes from Argos Panoptes, a hundred-eyed giant who served Hera, and whom Hermes slew to free a nymph coveted by Zeus. Panoptes's eyes slept in turns, so that some were always open, making him an excellent guard. But Hermes managed to put all hundred eyes to sleep by telling the giant boring stories.

Who watches the watchers? Why, we watch each other. You know, until we get bored.

Thinking of how many of my female friends set their Twitter profiles to "private." A gesture that could be read as both coquettish and self-protective—to cast the eyes down, at once to refuse a look and to limit what can be seen.

Or maybe they're just tired of curating only the most generically presentable selves. 15

The eyes are the social media platform of the soul?

Medusa defeats the male gaze by turning lookers-on into stone, and is in turn bested by a mirror.

Her example makes the female gaze seem essentially self-defeating. But there's also Diana, who turns peeping toms into deer and hunts them down.

Pedagogical theory tells us that books, like eyes, should act as both window and mirror—reflecting the reader while expanding her horizons.

But I've always thought of writing as a way of asserting control. 20

Adjusting *this* mirror. Drawing *that* curtain. Showing just what I want you to see.

A writer, too, should reflect a while before sending back images.

When Foucault wrote that "visibility is a trap," he meant for the person observed. But consider the wages of seeing: Turned to stone. Bored to death. Ripped to shreds.

What I mean is, you're getting off easy.

25   But what about me? Trying to catch your attention over the page's horizon, I may be showing more of myself than I mean.

The (Only) Good Fascist

I HAVE NEVER BEEN much good at ambiguity—a failing in a poet. I'm so bad at it, in fact, that when I was much younger, I jokingly referred to my work as "fascist poetics."

Of course, if we believe Slavoj Žižek, all poets are fascists.

This makes me think of something that Anthony Madrid wrote: "the trick is not so much to get rid of your vices, but to turn them to good account."

Here goes.

Writing on *Citizen*, Claudia Rankine's patient, accretive re- 5
counting of daily incidents of racism, Ben Lerner comments on the emotional "restraint, verging on flatness," of Rankine's prose.

But what choice does she have? Emotional flatness is one of the few rhetorical strategies available to a writer whose culture has made the open display of emotion—particularly in a woman of color—a sign of instability, a sign that her views should be dismissed.

And in a society disinclined to view her as truly human, why should a writer provide readers with her emotional labor?

Too, Richard Hugo identified an element of power play in emotionlessness, saying that there's "one rule for all who want the advantage over others: never show your feelings."

But I think that's a rule for those whose power isn't secure, who are trying to play the game from behind the eight ball. The truly powerful act wild without consequence. They think it's fun, in fact.

10   And things do look nicer through privilege-colored glasses.

Nicer, much nicer, but—ah, there's the rub: not perfect. You can be white, male, well-off, lauded in your career, and still your body can fail, your friends can die, your fame can rot, still you are just a little blip on the radar of time, a nothing against the background noise of the cosmos. And how are you going to face that?

Well, you might become a more compassionate person. Or, you might recede into the dream of control.

Philosophy professor Roderick T. Long writes that "according to Aristotle, feeling *less* anger than the situation calls for is as much a failure of moral perception as feeling *more*." And so a culture that permits emotion to be safely displayed by only a few traffics in distortion and error.

Carolyn Heilbrun puts it this way, "If one is not permitted to express anger or even to recognize it within oneself, one is, by simple extension, refused both power and control."

Citizen ends with the casualties of the dream of control: a litany of names, the names of Black men, women, children, all murdered. Each time a new edition is published, the list is longer. [15]

"Emotion in her is calcined to a thin ash," a reviewer wrote approvingly of Marianne Moore.

Where there's smoke, there's fire. And where there's ash, fire has passed.

"Paranoia is a weakness of the oppressed," according to Morgan Parker.

It also seems to be a weakness of the privileged, who fear the loss of their illusory control, while simultaneously accusing others of being out of control.

Things begin to seem a little circular. If we avoid reality by means of illusions that require real-world pain to sustain them, how can we ever get clear, to a point of unbiased perspective? [20]

In 1950, Archibald MacLeish wrote an imaginary dialogue in the wake of the controversy that erupted when Ezra Pound's

Pisan Cantos were awarded the Bollingen Prize. The dialogue argued that despite Pound's vile politics, his poem revealed the world as Pound perceived it, and thus accomplished the Aristotelian function of poetry as an instrument—however distorted—of knowledge.

Ariana Reines writes of Amiri Baraka: "I loved his rage. And rage is a danger to literature."

But why? Why is rage a danger to literature? Because it distorts truth? But per Aristotle, lack of rage may be just as much a distortion.

Perhaps it's because, as Jane McCabe once said, "through anger, the truth looks simple." And is the truth ever simple?

25   Here's what I think: *yes*. It's facing it that's hard.

Reines again: "I don't want to live in a culture too weak to learn from the fury it deserves."

In "The Rejection of Closure," Lyn Heijinian doesn't accept Žižek's assessment of poets. Instead, she asserts that a poet "challenges authority as a principle and control as a motive."

This, according to Mark Strand, is why people don't read poetry: "It suggests the possibility of loss of control right around the corner."

Well, maybe. But Wendell Berry describes poetry as a gate that "admit[s] only what is worth remembering." And so, as if to underscore Žižek's point, it must be poets who dictate what gets remembered.

But we all know that the victors write the history. And since when were poets the victors? ³⁰

Why did Ezra Pound write poetry? Why did Amiri Baraka? Why does Claudia Rankine? Lyn Heijinian? Wendell Berry? To assert control? To resist control? To admit the possibility of losing control or to recapture it?

I am not sure that a world without distinctions of race, gender, class, or disability would look much like this one. If such fundamental things were to change, surely other things would change as well.

A Bible verse I've always found disturbing—the one where Jesus says he gives peace, but "not as the world gives."

I mean, I'm used to the world. "As the world gives," I've largely been a success.

"Rulers," wrote Bertolt Brecht, "would like to see everything remain the same—for a thousand years if possible." ³⁵

What is truth?, asks Pontius Pilate. *It's what I'm telling you*, says every lawyer, fascist, poet, doctor, witness, prophet.

One of the central concerns of Aristotle's *Poetics* is catharsis, a word that originally referred to purging impurities from the body. Catharsis is the culmination of a process in which, as Hans-George Gadamer puts it, "the spectator . . . emerges with new insight from the illusions in which he, like everyone else, lives."

In an interview with Marc Maron, Sir Ian McKellen spoke of the difference he felt in his acting before and after he came out as gay. As he described it, acting stopped being a form of masquerade, a release for emotions he felt he wasn't allowed to have. Instead, acting became an art through which emotion—true emotion—was revealed.

Johanna Hedva writes that "a body is defined by its vulnerability." And we've all got a body.

40 This shared vulnerability could open a path forward. But mostly it seems to make us desperate.

This culminates in a truth that I arrive at and forget, arrive at and forget, so stark and unpleasant that it is a constant struggle to realize: cruelty arises in fear, and perpetuates itself in control.

Tone Police

THERE OUGHT TO BE a Miranda warning for life. You have the right to remain silent. Anything you say may be used against you.

Of course, remaining silent presents its own problems. For this reason, perhaps, my desire to express myself with absolute authority, control.

Here, for example, I have adopted a precise, removed, unemotional tone—the tone, I think, of a "reliable narrator." This writing is riddled with words like "per" and "therefore" and "of course" and "because"—the set dressing of reason.

And like any good lawyer, I've backed myself up with insistent quotation—appeals to authority.

Appeals to authority, according to classical logic, are among the least persuasive rhetorical strategies.

5

Olivia Laing describes loneliness as a condition that emerges not from being alone, but from a desire to be truly seen, coupled with the fear that others will hate what they see. Intimacy, by contrast, requires conditions in which it is safe to "reveal mistakes and imperfections."

But I don't desire intimacy. I desire certainty. I desire power and control.

In applying these desires to the act of writing, I think of the words that St. Augustine proposed for his epitaph: "When you read these words, I speak, and your voice is mine."

"Certainty is a type of performance," observes Michelle Detorie.

10 In *The Evasion-English Dictionary*, Maggie Balistreri writes that, "if I worry about your perception of me, it's probably because I did something to warrant it." But many people find that the only thing that they've done is have the wrong kind of body. Wrong color. Wrong sex. Dressed wrong, held wrong. Wonky eyes, legs, face, insides.

This subjects them to a scrutiny that reinscribes their difference, affirming that others, and not they, are in control.

Internet call-out culture tries to democratize this surveilling gaze, turning the scrutiny around: *We see you.*

As James Baldwin put it in a 1963 interview, "I have been described by you, for hundreds of years. And now, I can describe you. That's part of the panic."

It's a fair cop.

And the panic is real, if ultimately useless. A waste of energy, 15
Audre Lorde called it.

Like a body, language is always on the verge of failure, approximate. It both shows and it hides.

Robert Trivers explains it this way: "If one great virtue of language is its ability to make true statements about events distant in space and time, then surely one of its social drawbacks is its ability to make false statements about events distant in space and time."

For this reason, Tim Parks proposes that everyone read with pen in hand, annotating every text with questions, arguments, and rejections. In the absence of such disputatious reading, he complains that "sometimes it seems the whole of society languishes in the stupor of the fictions it has swallowed."

Alice Notley once observed wryly of male poets: "They've been brought up to have a good cover story."

One result of my careful, unemotional language is the erasure 20
of my body. But is it being erased for your sake? Or for mine?
Am I controlling myself, or being controlled?

Are there other bodies that this writing erases?

I think of Sueyeun Juliette Lee lamenting her own "disembodied 'objectivity'" in the face of Bhanu Kapil's *Ban en Banlieue*, a book that forces the reader to confront the consequences of the body's limitation and pain and subjection and subjectivity. And the particular consequences of the *wrong* body—unacceptably poor, broken, brown, female.

"The thing is that the aftereffects of trauma tend to hang around long after the stimulus is past," writes Laurie Penny.

In her 1971 essay, "Curriculum and Consciousness," Maxine Greene states that "it is by being unrestrictedly and unreservedly what I am at present that I have a chance of moving forward."

25 But how many of us are permitted to be "unrestrictedly and unreservedly" ourselves?

"If you are not risking sentimentality, you are not close to your inner self," wrote Richard Hugo.

But sentimentality, like selfhood, is a privilege. Safe indulgence is reserved for a few.

My even tone, avoiding sentimentality and vulnerability—it's a fascist way of proceeding. As though everything had to be impervious muscles and gleaming monoliths.

One could perhaps be forgiven, in this society, for feeling that this is all that it's acceptable to show.

Vivian Gornick describes Beryl Markham's memoir, *West* 30
with the Night, as steadily proceeding toward "... an open un-
derstanding of what lies beneath the need for impenetrable
self-protection": a fear of loneliness subordinated to a fear
that the self will not be loved, to the corresponding fear that
loving is weakness.

Remembering the title of a book that Claudia Rankine wrote
prior to *Citizen*: *Don't Let Me Be Lonely*.

As a writer, I want your attention but fear what you might
see. My reserved tone and insistent quotation take the light
off myself. This way, I draw your eye, but reflect your gaze
elsewhere.

"Don't look at me! I'm hideous!"

Ideally, being made aware of one's inattention, of one's erasing
of others, should lead to future attentiveness and sensitivity.
But that awareness—that sense of being scrutinized, of hav-
ing something to hide, often ends in a paroxysm of shame,
shame that gets covered over with more impervious muscles
and monoliths.

"Shame is a species of pride—crushed, inverted pride," writes 35
Christopher Nealon.

Quoting an unnamed teacher, Pema Chödrön explains that
"it's good that you feel that regret. . . . But you only get two

minutes for regret." After that, you have to do something about it.

Remembering a question asked of my husband at a Buddhist retreat: "When was the last time you were truly seen?" They seemed to think that being truly seen was a good thing. Of course, it could be both good and supremely discomfiting.

Audre Lorde called it "the intimacy of scrutiny." She argued that instead of becoming defensive under the gaze of others, we can use that gaze to free ourselves from "the fears which rule our lives and form our silences."

I don't want to think of myself as fearful or silent. But I'm not brave. I like comfort. I like safety. I'm not immune to our collective inheritance, the cold falsehoods that render us lonely and cruel. Actually, I've grown used to them.

40   Simone de Beauvoir wrote that, through her love of truth, she tore herself "away from the safe comfort of certainties," and that, in return, the truth rewarded her. But I am not sure that truth will reward me. I am not sure I am brave or good enough to perceive what the truth brings as a reward.

And so, is this anything, really, but a good cover story?

We see you we see you we see you.

And if it isn't anything more, how not to leave it there, to end in a paroxysm of shame, useless, monolithic? How to give up certainty and comfort for the stress—but also the great possibility—of a more equal, sentimental, and intimate world?

Moses Maimonides, glossing the Talmud: "Teach your tongue to say 'I don't know' and you shall progress."

"The more complex things are, the less certain the outcome but also the more room for the play of the mind, for inventing ourselves out of the mess," writes Joan Retallack.

Or as Dawn Lundy Martin puts it, "the prison does not allow for glee, but glee occurs anyway, on its own terms."

Could I find glee in turning the desire for order and certainty around, in refocusing it to some good account? Toward a world that acknowledges suffering, but strives equally for joy?

Maxine Greene concludes that "to plunge in; to choose; to disclose; to move: this is the road, it seems to me, to mastery." By "mastery," she means not control, but understanding.

And I remember how Audre Lorde defined "militancy": as the act of "fighting despair."

His Masterpiece

IN THE MIDDLE AGES, a story about Aristotle became very popular. It goes like this:

Aristotle advises his most famous pupil, Alexander the Great, to leave off all relations with women, the better to concentrate on statecraft. Spurned, Alexander's consort Phyllis sets out to get revenge by seducing Aristotle. Once the philosopher is completely besotted, Phyllis informs him that she'll submit to his advances only if he comes to her on all fours and lets her ride him around like a horse.

Aristotle goes for it.

I learned the facts of life after watching—yes, this is true—an episode of *The Facts of Life*. My mother evidently felt the show told me just enough about sex to get it wrong.

Once she filled me in on the birds and the bees, I was appalled, as any self-respecting eight-year-old would be. Still, I got over it.

Iris Murdoch once described Aristotle as the "Shakespeare of science." I take this to mean that, though Aristotle was not a scientist in any modern sense, he provided useful metaphors by which to get at the truth.

The "birds and the bees" isn't a metaphor but a euphemism, a circumlocution. Humans like those. We're not very good at facing facts. What we're good at is deciding that certain facts aren't worth our time.

Consider that while Aristotle understood that not just humans, but nearly all animals, reproduce sexually, this fact was virtually unknown among Europe's upper classes until the Enlightenment.

A well-bred Frenchman of the sixteenth century, for example, would have believed that mice just sort of spontaneously organize themselves out of garbage.

10   Emily Dickinson wrote that "The Truth must dazzle gradually / Or every man be blind." I'm not sure that she accepted, however, that we would often rather stay in the dark.

A refrain for human history: "I don't want to know, do I?"

"Confirmation bias" is the social psychologist's term for the tendency to cling to one's conclusions or opinions even more strongly when faced with contrary evidence. And so "I don't want to know" becomes "I refuse to know."

Capitalizing on the philosopher's medieval association with both ribaldry and esoteric knowledge, a popular Restoration-era sex manual and midwifery guide, which contained nothing written by Aristotle, was nonetheless titled *Aristotle's Masterpiece*.

Printed in multiple and various editions, copies of the *Masterpiece* were available in brown paper well into the 1900s. People still needed it, you see. It talked about things no one would talk about.

I used to know a guy who graduated from medical school without understanding how birth control pills—probably the most prescribed medication in America—actually work. In fact, he had little idea how any part of the female reproductive system functioned.

When I mention this to people who work in reproductive health, they're not surprised at all.

The second edition of *Aristotle's Masterpiece* lifted large chunks from an earlier guide to the amorous and reproductive arts, called *The Sick Woman's Private Looking-Glasse*.

That title embeds an idea that continues with us today—the notion that sexual matters, and specifically those of women, are a kind of private sickness, that there's no need for anyone—including women themselves, ideally—to know about.

15

"We have been a little insane about the truth," wrote Wallace Stevens. He was talking about poetry, but he could have been talking about, well, all aspects of human endeavor.

20   Preparing for the weeklong mission of the first female astronaut, NASA engineers asked Sally Ride if one hundred tampons would be the right number to include in the ship's stores. No, she informed them, that would not be the right number.

When I first read this story, I laughed in disbelief. But at least the engineers asked. They appear to have been more concerned with getting it right than looking foolish.

Still, they look pretty foolish. That's how learning works.

In an essay on literary explorations of interpersonal intimacy, Julia Obert argues that while curiosity is necessary to true knowledge, it must be tempered with vulnerability if it is to be of any use.

In other words, to know another, you must expose yourself. You must give up the pretense of control.

25   The story of Phyllis and Aristotle was meant to warn young scholars from female company. But the story could easily be read with other morals in mind.

Remember: Aristotle fails to take his own advice. I like to think it was his curiosity, and not his lust, that got him on his knees.

Metaphor as Illness

ILLNESS IS NOT an event; it is a condition.

We would like it to be an event, a progression that ends in a cure.

But disease is apt to waver, wander, to spiral in circles, refusing to end unless—until—you do.

In addition to being diagnosed with AZOOR, and having troubles with blue lights appearing randomly in my vision, I have had unexplained scarring on my left cornea for more than twenty years.

The optometrist who first noticed the scarring, like every eye doctor I've seen since, gave me an Amsler grid to take home and put on the fridge.

An Amsler grid resembles a piece of graph paper with a large dot in the middle. You're supposed to stare at the dot with one eye closed and note whether any of the surrounding lines look wavy, blurred, or are absent. It is a self-test for macular degeneration.

All these blind spots and lights and grids feel like metaphors for how, when I try to ignore things, or hide them from myself, they have a way of popping up unbidden.

"The body's treachery is thought to have its own inner logic," wrote Susan Sontag in *Illness as Metaphor*. By means of this magical thinking, disease is correlated, in a funhouse mirror sort of way, with character.

I'm a poet, so of course I have a metaphorically inflected disease.

10   Virginia Woolf once wondered at how few literary works explore, or even acknowledge, the bodily realities of illness. Instead, she observed, "literature does its best to maintain that . . . the body is a sheet of plain glass through which the soul looks straight and clear."

As Anne Boyer puts it, "I've read some books, thus my ambivalence about literature."

In the late 1700s, a charlatan oculist calling himself "Chevalier" John Taylor traveled throughout Europe in a coach painted with the sign of an eye and a Latin inscription meaning "Who gives sight gives life." As part of his peripatetic practice, he is said to have treated Bach and Handel, and is thought to have blinded them both.

After a long career of botching cataract surgeries and maiming musical geniuses, Taylor himself died blind.

As Wallace Stevens wrote, "reality is a cliché."

Stevens pointed to metaphor as the escape hatch. But philos- 15
ophers from Aristotle to Derrida have argued that the point
of metaphor is not to escape reality, but to expose, amplify,
and reveal it. Even if—and perhaps precisely because—un-
mediated reality can never be precisely pinned down.

After reading about the Chevalier, I am grateful that there
is no invasive treatment—or any treatment—prescribed for
AZOOR. As an article in the *American Journal of Ophth-
almology* drily concludes, "the value of treatment is uncertain."

To quote every mother everywhere, "It won't get better unless
you leave it alone."

The word *metaphor* literally means to carry over, or transfer,
as in transferring the characteristics of one thing to another,
naming one thing as another.

These transfers are not always obvious. As the analytic phi-
losopher Max Black wrote, metaphor "disappear[s] when it
is successful."

The body, too, goes unnoticed—a mere platform or container 20
in which our brains move around and we have sex—until it
does something inconvenient.

It is, of course, nearly always doing something inconvenient.

The discovery of my blind spots came after I sought help for blurry vision. Because the blind spots were the focus of many subsequent appointments, I assumed that they were the cause of my blurry vision.

About five visits in, I mentioned this to my doctor, who explained that there was no way that the blind spots would cause the rest of my visual field to blur. "Looks like nothing we've been doing in any way addresses that!" he said cheerfully.

All very understandable, really. The blind spots were confirmable and could be tested. Blurry vision, though? Anything could cause that.

25 And anyway, the blurring cleared up by itself over time.

George Lakoff and Mark Johnson point out that many common English phrases describe arguments in terms of warfare: debaters maintain entrenched positions, fend off counterattacks, and launch decisive blows.

This metaphorical frame is so familiar that we hardly notice how such phrasing discounts the degree to which arguments are not like battles, or don't have to be.

I've noticed something in the past few years. I'll glance at a sign and my mind will report back something totally different than what the sign actually says. Is this a symptom of my eye problems—that my brain is trying to fill in missing information? Or is it just a symptom of my personality—restless, jumping to conclusions?

I hate going to the doctor but, like many anxious people, I'm convinced that my every itch, twitch, and bump is the sign of some terrible and fatal problem.

Although he sometimes makes tender light of this tendency, 30
my husband's the one who sent me to the doctor when, several years before my blurry vision and AZOOR diagnosis, I complained of seeing blue lights before my eyes.

Multiple doctor's appointments and disturbing tests later, the conclusion was: You see blue lights before your eyes.

At the time that Susan Sontag wrote *Illness as Metaphor*, cancer sufferers were thought to be frigid, uptight people whose inability to emote had caused their insides to curdle.

Such a metaphorical frame is unthinkable now, when the disease's most public faces are mothers fighting breast cancer and children with leukemia.

Instead, we envision cancer patients as warriors who will not flag or stop or falter, who refuse to negotiate with this terrorist disease.

But cancer isn't a terrorist. It has no ideology. Cancer is lit- 35
erally a mistake, an ungoverned multiplication of cells. You don't fight a mistake; you correct it.

But mistake's another metaphor—one which, if adopted, would place blame on those patients whose cancers prove "uncorrectable."

I am dismayed by the metaphor inherent in the very word "patient," that sense of someone waiting for the duration. I am an impatient.

In Aristotle's view, metaphor is superior to literal expression precisely because it is beguiling. By inviting us to compare dissimilar objects, metaphor appeals to humanity's love of solving puzzles, of uncovering the hidden.

But for every successful uncovering, there may be a false exchange, a dubious correspondence, a wrongheaded solution.

40   Why take these kinds of chances?

In a 1667 book that influenced the development of scientific writing, Thomas Sprat implored the members of the Royal Academy of London to avoid metaphorical descriptions, and instead to precisely describe observed phenomena.

After all, as Lyn Heijinian put it 300 years later, "can a tropical shoreline or a turning iceberg ever usefully be said to be 'like' anything?"

Aristotle thought so, if the metaphor was right. Of course, he probably also thought he was making sense when he compared dreams to the red haze a menstruating woman's gaze leaves on a mirror.

AZOOR is a metaphor for the same thing for which all diseases are symbol and sign—the condition of being alive.

Some metaphors for you: Being afraid is like being alive. 45
Being in pain is like being alive. Being uncertain is like being alive.

"Living is a form of not being sure, not knowing what next or how," said Agnes de Mille. "We take leap after leap in the dark."

But that doesn't mean we can't hunt for the light switch.

Another metaphor there. The conflation of light with knowledge and reason.

Even the word *idea* comes from the ancient Greek *eido*, meaning "to see." We perceive invisible ideas by the unreal rays of an imagined sun.

Recounting a news item, my husband tells me that scien- 50
tists have implanted a memory in a mouse. They have made it think that it received an electric shock in one room when, really, it received a shock in another, totally differently room. It now reacts with dismay to the "wrong" room.

In one sense, this story is not metaphorical. There were actual scientists, an actual mouse, and an actual experiment in which the mouse was made to recall something differently than it happened.

But in the sense that the story took place in a world that we understand solely by the medium of human consciousness, it is nothing but metaphor, a parable loaded with symbols, signs, portents, and premonitions.

In "Professions for Women," Virginia Woolf describes two problems confronting any woman writer. First, she must strangle the "Angel in the House"—the collective voices, internal and external, that tell her not to try at all. Woolf writes that although she solved this problem for herself, each woman must solve it again on her own terms.

But "the second [problem], telling the truth about my own experiences as a body, I do not think I solved. I doubt that any woman has solved it yet."

55   Sidney Bradford, a machinist in his fifties who was blind from childhood, was one of the first recipients of a cornea transplant. Although he regained his sight, he became unable to work, confused by the look of objects he had formerly manipulated solely by touch. He committed suicide two years later.

Or he may have just died after a long illness. The accounts I have read of Bradford's life state that it was either one or the other, but disagree as to which.

Where the accounts agree, however, is that the cure was worse than the disease.

Illness is obscene in its reality. No wonder we hurry to clothe it in metaphor, to drape it in woolly lengths of symbolism.

"Just let me slip into something a little more comfortable."

According to Joanna Bourke, "bodies [in pain] are not simply entities awaiting social inscription." They are "active agents in both creating social worlds and, in turn, being created by them." 60

Language is an instrument of this creation. As Martha King observes, "words are intrinsically connected to one's body."

And always inadequate to the task of approximating or fixing into place the reality around us. As Derrida has it, language is spoken from a position of blindness.

Borges went blind. So did Milton. And Bach. And Monet. And Handel. And Galileo.

In *The Society of the Spectacle*, Guy Debord quotes Ludwig Feuerbach as stating that "the highest degree of illusion [is] the highest degree of sacredness."

Borges agreed, opining that representing silence with the noise of three military bands is more intelligent, sophisticated, artistic, and valuable than representing silence with silence. 65

But silence isn't merely similar to silence. It *is* silent.

And Joyce. And Degas.

Because our language is approximate, "[we] must," writes Derrida, "expose [our]selves, run through space as if running a risk."

In transferring the qualities of one thing to another, every metaphor necessarily marks a divide, saying *this is the way across.*

70   Thereby implicitly denying that there is any other.

Among metaphor's risks—that we will perceive similarities without substance, distinctions without difference.

And the way that we perceive things matters.

During the Battle of Copenhagen, the future Lord Nelson, having previously been blinded in one eye, ignored a lieutenant's news that he was being signaled to fall back. Placing his spyglass against his blind eye, he blandly stated, "I really do not see the signal."

If Nelson had lost that battle, his story would be a cautionary tale of the consequences of ignoring reality.

75   But he won.

We perceive nothing directly, or clearly, without the intervention of mind, memory, metaphor. And yet we run the risk. We call 'em like we see 'em.

The least we can do is look hard.

Dispatch from the Uncanny Valley

.

IN HIS 1869 INAUGURAL ADDRESS as the president of Harvard College, Charles Eliot dismissed suggestions that the institution become coeducational, opining that the innate differences between men and women rendered the latter unsuitable for higher education.

One hundred and forty years later, one President of Harvard echoed another, as Larry Summers pronounced the varying graduation rates for men and women in scientific disciplines as being due to innate differences.

For many years, I assumed that all prejudice was the result of ignorance, that knowledge would erase it. Familiarity, I presumed, would breed respect.

But that's not how the saying goes, is it?

And if prejudice really were the result of ignorance, how could misogyny exist? Women are hard to avoid.

Another assumption of mine, one that I suppose that

5

presidents of Harvard do not share—when you get right down to it, men and women are really very much the same.

In 1970, Japanese researchers noted that the more human a robot's appearance and behavior, the more easily humans will interact with it. Up to a point. Acceptance dips sharply when a robot looks and acts almost nearly, but not exactly, like a natural person.

At this point—termed the "uncanny valley"—the robot is like one of those optical illusions that at first seems to be a vase, and then a pair of faces. The ambiguity causes observers intense discomfort.

Are they looking at a machine or a human? At something that is neither or both?

10   Whatever it is, it's creepy.

In the name of overcoming our discomfort with those who are different from us, we are often asked to have empathy, to focus on our similarities.

But as Hari Ziyad puts it, "I will never be my sisters, and if their only worth is how much of me I can see in them, there is far too much of them that is worthless."

Too, the notion that similarity begets civility assumes that we like things that are like ourselves. But according to the psychologist D. W. Winnicott, misogyny stems from men's disgust at their own vulnerability. When "traced to its root in the history of each individual, this fear of WOMAN turns out to be a fear of recognizing the fact of dependence."

I also fear dependence. But to paraphrase Eve Kosofsky Sedgwick, fear knows some things well and other things poorly.

One of the things it knows poorly is the impossibility—for anyone—of control.

If empathy won't serve, another option is to trust that others and their experiences are valid, even when we don't understand them.

This seems to me to be a call for kindness.

"Kindness," as Adam Phillips and Barbara Taylor define it, is "the ability to bear the vulnerability of others and therefore of oneself."

I, for one, am terrible at it.

Could you be kind to a monster? Could you be kind to a robot? Could you be kind to a woman?

A harder question, perhaps: could you be kind to yourself?

To extend trust is to have a kind of faith. Having been taught to take nothing on faith, I am uncomfortable with this.

But I am already uncomfortable, cautious and concerned about others' motivations, just as they may be cautious and concerned about mine. There are a lot of words for this—*oppressive, exhausting*—but what it isn't is *fun*.

Here's a quote often attributed to Lenin, and which my husband's German dentist once favored him with, while wrist-deep in his mouth: "Trust is good. Control is better."

25   Is an illusion better than reality?

I once wrote a poem called "The Worst That Could Happen." The worst was to be afraid. And I am afraid.

And so, I should be able to come out from under all illusions, do anything, live any way at all, right? With nothing left to lose?

Oh, little girl. There's always something left to lose.

Recalling the debate I had with myself over whether to retweet two tweets that asked you (please) to retweet if you were a woman and had been followed by a man in public and grabbed by a strange man in public.

30   I am a woman who has been followed by a man in public, and grabbed by a strange man in public. But I didn't want to

retweet because I didn't want to admit that I was vulnerable in this way, that I had not been able to keep these things from happening.

I also know that refusing to admit these things gives the jerks who do them license to continue with impunity.

I get annoyed whenever someone suggests that women just take self-defense classes. I don't want to be grabbed and then kick a guy's ass. I want to not be grabbed in the first place.

I have long had friends who might be described as "free spirits." They do drugs; they go hiking naked in the woods with handsome men; they take spontaneous trips to Thailand. They hurl themselves at life with the enthusiasm of concert crowd-surfers, sure that collective kindly hands will buoy them aloft.

I have always thought these people stupid.

Paranoia teaches us that there is always more to be afraid of, but also that there are always more ways to forestall pain. Ways to dress, ways not to go out, car keys to hold fixed in your hand like claws, hotlines to call. So that pain happens not to the unlucky, but to those who deserve it, to those who weren't paranoid enough.

I have noticed in myself a reaction when I read news accounts of victimization, particularly sexual victimization.

35

My instinct is not so much to help the innocent as to punish the guilty. It is an instinct I distrust in myself, because I know where it comes from.

Never forget the person who made you feel vulnerable and never stop punishing yourself for it. Others for it. Never stop.

Catharine MacKinnon famously advocated the abolition of privacy laws, reasoning that in practice they were only used to veil the abuses of male aggressors, while leaving women totally exposed. So why not admit that openly, and turn the exposure around?

40   You who have made us so visible, understand this: visibility is only painful if you have something to hide.

But we all have something to hide. Or maybe, something we shouldn't be forced to show. Or the display of which we should be permitted to control.

Too, we all have things we should be forced to acknowledge.

I've spent a lifetime with what Sedgwick identifies as a paranoiac's mantra: *There must be no bad surprises. There must be no bad surprises.*

Bad surprises have happened anyway.

On the subway, on the street, once in a medical office, a cou- 45
ple of nurses bursting into a room, pulling the doctor off
and away.

Still, as Sedgwick mildly observes, if bad surprises are possi-
ble, so are good ones.

When I first read this observation, it excited me as a poten-
tial way out of fear's trap, a metaphorical and metaphysical
swerve. I thought it would help me to believe in the potential
for an interpersonal intimacy that could withhold despair.

I got kind of starry-eyed about the whole thing, in fact.

And then we had a presidential election.

Sitting alone in my house at three in the morning, drinking 50
rye, on November 9, 2016, I have never felt so uncanny.

Julia Obert notes that because we cannot be each other, we
can never be sure we understand each other, no matter how
hard we try.

For example, even if I read all the books there are on octo-
pi, and get a PhD in octopi studies, I won't be an octopus.
Likewise, I will never be Black; I cannot be chromosomally
male. I cannot be a second-generation immigrant, or have
spina bifida, or have been born somewhere other than a naval
hospital in Rhode Island.

But, as Obert argues, the irreducibility of others is, paradoxically, one of the foundations of intimacy. You are not the same as me. And I am not the same as you. But if we both accept and respect this fact, we can accept and respect each other.

In 1908, Nebraska schoolteacher Leta Hollingworth moved with her husband to New York City so that he could pursue a graduate degree. She then learned that local law forbade married women from teaching school. So she went and got a graduate degree herself.

55   For her dissertation project, Hollingworth disproved the theory of functional periodicity, which posited that women were utterly incapacitated, both physically and mentally, during menstruation. Much in vogue at the time, the theory was used to support women's exclusion from various kinds of education, jobs, and civic roles.

With no offense to Hollingworth, the theory was pretty easy to disprove. It didn't square with almost anyone's experience of almost any woman.

But to paraphrase Shawn Hamilton, the fact that it needed to be disproved demonstrates the relative power of the people who treated it as true. It demonstrates that their interest lay not in truth or falsity, but in emphasizing the otherness of women.

In 2017, Larry Summers—the same Larry Summers who several years before had questioned women's mental aptitude for scientific and technological disciplines—wrote that he was distancing himself from challenges to "political correctness."

Explaining that there had been a rash of anti-Semitic incidents at his daughters' schools, he argued that such challenges only licensed bigotry.

According to the *Harvard Business Review*, of all possible publications, vulnerability is a characteristic of lifelong learners. 60

Speaking as someone who has spent her life trying to foreclose her vulnerabilities, being vulnerable means learning a lot of things you never wanted to know.

To quote Ecclesiastes: "He that increaseth knowledge increaseth sorrow."

Being kind to others means being open to the possibility you're being played for a sucker. It means making yourself vulnerable.

Asking someone to choose vulnerability and its discomforts in the name of fairness, freedom, learning, or intimacy, is asking them for courage. It's a big ask.

Of course, we usually don't ask for this sacrifice in a vacuum 65
of free choice. Uncanniness is the birthright of many, for the benefit of the few.

In her essay "Becoming Ugly," Madeleine Davies explains that she had no interest in moving past her own rage and grief in the wake of the 2016 election, instead preferring to "become as repulsive as I can in an insult to these men—so many men—who hate women and the women who adulate them."

Seems reasonable to me. I mean, if society persists in treating you as strange and alien no matter what you do, then you might as well be the monster you want to see in the world.

That doesn't mean there's nothing left to lose. It just means acknowledging that you don't control whether the loss occurs.

All you control is the sort of person who confronts the loss.

70 My mother once mused to me that she would like her epitaph to read something along these lines: *She tried her best*. I'd like to live up to that myself.

And I can't say the world doesn't hand out opportunities like candy.

The monster I want to see in the world has technicolor antennae, laser eyes, and speaks French. She is kinder and braver than I am.

I'm not that monster, and might never be. But when I look in the mirror, I think I can catch a shiver, a tinge. I can see what might happen if I really tried.

A Likely Story

I AM THINKING AGAIN about T. S. Eliot's idea that writing is a means of escape. I love this idea and I hate it. I love it, because I'd like to escape. I hate it, because escape is false.

And while reality may be difficult to face, it at least has the virtue of being real.

Despite its hallucinatory qualities.

Two thousand years after Aristotle told us that women's menstrual cycles can change the color of mirrors, Oliver Sacks noted the lack of any portion of the brain charged with "ensuring the truth, or at least the veridical character, of our recollections."

As Jessica Smith writes, "our memories do not conform to linear narratives." Instead, we remember "fragmentary colors, patterns, and little snippets." And so, "to narrativize [a] memory is to fill in the gaps."

5

How many times have I been tested now for colorblindness? Four? Three?

You might think that writing things down would be a good solution. But ancient scholars believed it only made things worse, by giving everyone an excuse not to commit things to memory. And once people became unable to recall events accurately of their own accord, they also lost the ability to tell truth from falsehood.

They came to trust what is written even though anyone can write anything at all.

After my AZOOR diagnosis, I had periodic appointments to remap my blind spots, so that my doctor could chart the progress of the disease. For two and a half years, the blind spots did not change. Three years after my diagnosis, the tests revealed that they were gone.

10   Gone?

I don't recall this ever having been presented to me as a possibility. Instead, I understood that the blind spots would either stay the same, or more probably, get bigger.

For three years, I thought of myself as partially blind, maybe going all the way. And then I wasn't. Was anything ever wrong with me at all?

"I am half sick of shadows," said the Lady of Shalott.

In her memoir *The Red Parts*, Maggie Nelson writes that she became a poet instead of a novelist because of her distrust of narrative. I would love to be a novelist, to lie for my living. But I can't write dialogue, character, or plot.

So I write arguments instead. 15

But an argument, like a story, is a way of saying what happened, of saying what's important about it, of saying there's nothing else to know.

My husband thinks that I never had AZOOR, that my doctor perceived the zebras of a rare disease where there were only the everyday horses of eyestrain.

But what of the fact that I still see blue spots before my eyes, that pulsating chevrons occasionally overtake my vision, beginning from the lower right-hand side and slowly moving up and over my entire line of sight?

Consider also the fact, now baffling even to myself, that when my doctor told me I had a rare disease that could cause me to go blind, I never got a second opinion.

Am I committed to the truth, or to the story? 20

In *The Defense of Poesy*, Sir Philip Sidney argued that poetry improves on reality, giving us examples of virtue superior to those we find in real life. And so art is delusion, but a morally useful one.

There's a slippery slope: the good lie. The upright untruth. No wonder Plato had rather be done with it.

Here is Derrida's explanation as to why he accepted, unhesitatingly, an invitation to contribute an essay in memorial after the death of Michel Foucault: "Above all, because I love memory. This is nothing original, of course, and yet, how else can one love?"

There's a wistful quality in that statement, as if Derrida were admitting a weakness. But is the weakness in memory, or in love?

25   Borges wrote that "We are our memory ... that mountain of broken mirrors."

Or maybe not. Psychologists used to think that narrative memory was the basis of identity—lose your memories, lose your self. But more recent studies suggest that it is the capacity for moral reasoning, and not any specific narrative of past events, that gives each of us an "I."

In college, I jokingly referred to my double major in Spanish Culture and Russian Civilization, which involved taking classes on the Holy Inquisition, the Spanish Civil War, the Stalinist Terrors, and the Gulag Archipelago, as "torture studies."

These classes were a continuation of something I had believed since childhood: that if I read about enough bad things,

I would be inoculated against evil. I would be forewarned; I would become a good person.

But all that reading fed another side of me as well, the side that, in Jenny Offill's words, "thinks instead of acts. A character flaw, not a virtue."

Camille Dungy writes of her exasperation with white liberals' disbelief and dismay after the 2016 election, noting that "black people have been pointing out that 'this' is actually happening" forever.

"This" being a world that doesn't conform to your hopes, your expectations, to what you considered the common reality.

In *The Interpretation of Dreams*, Freud glosses an old joke about a man who is being sued for damaging a borrowed kettle. The man defends himself by simultaneously arguing that he didn't damage the kettle, that it was already damaged when he borrowed it, and that he never borrowed it anyway.

Dreams work like this, Freud argues, smoothly melding incompatible concepts without our raising the least objection.

Power works like this as well, requiring acceptance of more and more inconsistencies. It lacks rules and decency.

I've spent much of my life operating under what Aleksandar Hemon calls "the ontological blankie of reality inertia." Things are and have been a certain way, and if they change, it will be in ways that I find understandable.

But as the world changes in ways I find incomprehensible, I've started to consider a fundamental question: What exactly are my convictions?

Aristotle's statement about menstruating women and mirrors could have been tested, even in ancient Greece. They had mirrors, before which one might parade any number of menstruating and nonmenstruating women and record the results.

That's not to say that Aristotle was lying, when he wrote that the gaze of a menstruating woman turns mirrors red.

But let's keep in mind that the difference between *lying* and *being mistaken* is in intent, not effect.

40   Brian Blanchfield's book *Proxies* comprises a series of essays based solely on Blanchfield's unaided recollection. Each essay begins with an acknowledgment that it "permit[s] shame, error, guilt, myself the single source."

I appreciate Blanchfield's openness and vulnerability, his calling attention to our "susceptibility to error." But I have become a little obsessed with ensuring the accuracy of the dozens of quotations here. With fact-checking. As of today, I'm up to twenty-three pages of endnotes.

According to Keats, "Negative Capability . . . is when man is capable of being in uncertainties. Mysteries, doubts, without any irritable reaching after fact and reason."

He thought it was a hallmark of genius. But I don't want to be in uncertainties. I hate uncertainties.

As I checked over the first drafts of what you are reading now, I found rampant misquotes, false attributions, stuff that was totally backwards. I was tempted to leave it alone. After all, like Borges or Lewis Carroll, I've always loved reversals and mirroring, and the strange correspondences that resulted from my errors felt beautiful in this way.

When I was a teenager, I lied a lot. I was good at it. But I stopped after a while. Not because lying was wrong. But because I caught myself believing my own lies.

And that ability—that power—frightened me. Since that time, my goal has been zero negative capability.

My mind and memory are imperfect instruments, just like my eyes. But that doesn't mean I can't make an effort to backstop them. That doesn't mean I can't be alert to correction.

Masha Gessen writes that, in a totalitarian state, "lying is the message," an attempt "to assert power over truth itself." For the totalitarian, a persistent sense of unreality is a feature, not a bug.

I'm trying to get something across to myself. I'm trying to say something about freedom and control, about knowledge and truth and memory. Still, by now you're probably thinking that I just keep going on and on and on.

50   "Do I repeat myself? Very well, then, I repeat myself."

Anyway, that's life for you. It just keeps going on and on and on.

Until it doesn't.

My motive for trying to distinguish truth from falsity, as best I can tell, is an old one.

It's not that I think that life has a grand meaning, though that would be nice. I just mean that life isn't actually a dream.

55   It's real, and that reality is shared. This is both the best and the worst thing about it.

Here are some statements of fact: As I write this sentence, I am on my period. It is January 20, 2017.

I am afraid; I am imperfect; I make mistakes; I am unkind and fearful and I remember things wrong. Tomorrow I will go marching, despite feeling that I don't deserve to, that I've been too weak, that everything is hopeless, that I am uncertain of what is going on, despite all of this.

My conviction is that we are bad at perceiving truth, and worse at accepting it. But there is truth anyway. Reality exists. And knowing that, it can change.

Ceci n'est pas un fin.

Envoi: The Marvelous

It's January, a few years later. I am menstruating again.

A bit earlier than I'd like. I had an IUD put in a while back, and since then my periods have been all over the map.

I got the IUD because I had to discontinue the pill. I had to discontinue the pill because I had a pulmonary embolism.

A bunch of them, really. On the CAT scan, my lungs looked like a miniature delta pocked with boulders.

All of this happened in Maine, where I moved in June 2017.   5

In addiction literature, "pulling a geographic" means upping stakes and going somewhere new. It can act as a form of self-therapy, in that the practical questions of finding a place to live and learning new routines take precedence over the deeply grounded problems that cause the addictive behavior.

The therapeutic effects, however, are limited.

It's from a room with a view of an ancient, shaggy white spruce, serenaded by the constant sound of lawn mowers in summer and snowblowers in winter, that I've watched statues pulled down, women run over, children put into camps, impeachment hearings, the aftermath of more mass shootings than I can count, and the confirmation of a Supreme Court justice who thinks the pill works by causing abortions. Soon enough—though I don't know it yet—I'll see a pandemic, the Black Lives Matter movement, and the overturn of *Roe v. Wade*.

To set one thing straight, the pill doesn't cause abortion. Occasionally, however, it may result in blood clots.

10   The past few years have left me less enamored of citations, no longer certain that hard facts can save the day, that evidence and reason are enough.

As the sociologist Tressie McMillan Cottom has said, "you can't beat an ideology with evidence. The ideology controls the rules of evidence, not the other way around."

And if that's the case, what options are left for moving forward, changing anything for the better?

The artists that made up the Dada and Surrealist movements came of age during World War I and its aftermath. They roundly rejected reason as a means of positive change. Reason, after all, had blown up all of Europe.

Nearly dying, too, has a way of opening the mind to things that can't be boiled down to logic.

After I was discharged from the hospital, I researched pulmonary embolisms. One of the symptoms, I learned, is a feeling of dread. 15

That made me laugh. I mean, how would I distinguish that from my normal existence?

And yet, despite a continuous stream of enraging and depressing events, I don't feel nearly as much despair as I think would be sensible. Maybe it's that, as Nikki Wallschlaeger puts it, "I would rather encourage survival than prepare for extinction."

When my husband told his cousin, a nurse practitioner, about the embolisms, she mentioned that Serena Williams has had them repeatedly. After she developed new embolisms while giving birth, her doctors didn't believe her at first about the symptoms.

Yet another addition to the stuffed-to-the-gills-and-still-coming genre of medical professionals nearly killing a woman by not listening to what she has to say about her body.

That isn't my story, though. Mine is the story of a woman who nearly killed herself by not listening to her body. 20

When you have embolisms, your lungs work fine. Air goes in, air goes out. But your blood can't get through the clots to pick up oxygen, preventing you from making any use of the air.

For about two weeks before I was hospitalized, it was as if I'd forgotten how to breathe. I gasped on conference calls; I got winded climbing the stairs.

I tried to walk it off by taking long hikes. Twenty years of education and zero common sense.

My husband finally convinced me to go to a doctor when it started to hurt to breathe. The doctor thought I might have some kind of bug, but ordered a test to rule out clots.

25 Within twenty-four hours, I'd been admitted to the hospital, wheeled into a CAT scan, diagnosed, and was back home with a six-month prescription for blood thinners, a new oxygen monitor from the local drugstore, and a sensation of bewildered after-fright at how death came close enough to touch, and then swerved away.

I don't even have a scar to show you. But I do have this realization: when my life was in danger and I wasn't taking care of myself, others stepped in to do it for me. Efficiently, kindly.

Not everyone gets that. But I did.

What is the appropriate emotion in the face of something inexplicable, senseless, something so strange?

"An epiphany can emerge slowly," writes Mark Nowak.

It took months for me to be able to walk any distance 30
without sending my pulse soaring and my oxygen levels dangerously low.

But when I was able to take walks again, I found myself in an old orchard maintained by the local Audubon Society, among lichen-spattered stones carved with memorial phrases, benches with memorial plaques.

And then tears on the sudden. Packed-away fear tumbling out of the attic, suffused with pleasure in walking, in reading the names. In being there. Being anywhere.

I remain a partisan of reason, of evidence. But I don't mean to disdain any tool at my disposal.

As the English surrealist David Gascoyne put it, "The marvelous is within everyone's reach."

My perspective is necessarily limited. I don't know what I 35
don't know, and I don't know things that I should. And so I wonder if you should really be reading this. I mean, you should be reading everything. But this?

Thanks for being kinder to me than I deserved.

Though that's what kindness is.

And if anything here makes you say *naaaahhhh, not for me, come back later after you've done your homework, lady,* I get it.

But you do have to live in this world with me. And I get to live in this world with you.

40   Lucky us?

Yes, I think. Lucky half-sighted, gasping, enraged, humble, hopeless, still-going-on us. Can you feel how we flicker and stir? How we're closer than we appear?

NOTES

While every effort has been made to ensure that all citations are accurate at the time of publication, the internet is not a very stable archive. For a clickable list of many of these sources, go to: https://bloofbooks.com/notes-on-dreams.

Epigraph

Aristotle, *On Dreams*, trans. J. I. Beare, http://classics.mit. edu/Aristotle/dreams.html.

Preface: On *On Dreams*

Statement 4: Margaret Thomson Janvier, "The Sandman," *Poets.org*, https://www.poets.org/poem/sandman.

Statement 6: William Shakespeare, *Hamlet*, act 3, sc. 2.

Statement 7: Jay M. Enoch, "History of Mirrors Dating Back 8000 Years," *Optometry & Vision Science*, vol. 83, no. 10 (2006): 775–81; the Metropolitan Museum of Art, "Bronze mirror with a support in the form of a draped woman," https://www.metmuseum.org/ art/collection/search/255391; Katy Kelleher, "The Ugly History of Beautiful Things: Mirrors," *Longreads* (Jul. 11, 2019), https://longreads.com/2019/07/11/ the-ugly-history-of-beautiful-things-mirrors/.

Statement 8: Rosamond Kent Sprague, "Aristotle on Red Mirrors (On Dreams II 459b24-460a23)," *Phronesis*, vol. 30, no. 3 (1985): 323–25, https://www.jstor.org/stable/4182237.

Statement 9: Aristotle, *History of Animals*, trans. D'Arcy Wentworth Thompson, bk. 2, pt. 3, http://classics.mit.edu/Aristotle/history_anim.2.ii.html.

Statement 12: Ovid, *The Metamorphoses*, trans. Horace Gregory (Signet Classics, 2009), 74–75.

Statement 15: Doug posted these reminiscences, as best as I can tell from my Facebook activity log, sometime in the summer of 2012. However, they have since been removed, so you'll just have to trust me.

Statement 18: Danielle Pafunda, "Who Gets the Girl: A Note on Possession Flicks: Drawing Heavily on Kate Durbin's Demon Notions, My Favorite Movies When I Was 10, and Some Other Stuff," *Delirious Hem* (Jan. 9, 2013), https://delirioushem.blogspot.com/2013/01/who-gets-girl-note-on-possession-flicks.html; Beckian Fritz Goldberg, "Poetry and Murder" in *Planet on the Table; Poets on the Reading Life*, eds. Sharon Bryan and William Olsen (Sarabande Books, 2003), 173; Matt Simon, "Fantastically Wrong: The Theory of the Wandering Wombs That Drove Women to Madness," *Wired* (May 7, 2014), https://www.wired.com/2014/05/fantastically-wrong-wandering-womb/.

Statement 20: Emily Dickinson, "Tell all the truth but tell it slant," *Poetry Foundation*, https://www.poetryfoundation.org/poems/56824/tell-all-the-truth-but-tell-it-slant-1263; 1 Corinthians 13:12 (King James Version).

Statement 21: T. S. Eliot, *Four Quartets*, "Burnt Norton," pt. 1, lns. 44–45.

Statement 22: The sense of semantic derangement I experienced upon first encountering this phrase (in a regulatory guidance document issued by US Customs and Border Protection) has stuck with me for two decades. As a gesture toward clarity, it fails completely. But as an example of how difficult it can be to know, much less express, the truth, this phrase fits the bill. For an example of it in its native habitat, see US Customs and Border Protection, *What Every Member of the Trade Community Should Know About: U.S. Rules of Origin* (May 2004) page 4, https://www.cbp.gov/sites/default/files/assets/documents/2020-Feb/ICP-US-Rules-of-Origin-2014-Final.pdf.

The Woman, the Mirror, the Eye

Statement 5: Plutarch, *On Superstition*, trans. F. C. Babbitt, https://penelope.uchicago.edu/Thayer/E/Roman/Texts/Plutarch/Moralia/De_superstitione*.html. Plutarch ascribed the saying to Heraclitus. This is an early example of the infuriating tendency of quotations to wander from writer to writer. The translation used here is found in Joseph Addison, *The Spectator*, no. 487 (Sep. 18, 1712), https://www.gutenberg.org/files/12030/12030-h/12030-h.htm#section487. For Macnish's statement, see Robert Macnish, *The Philosophy of Sleep* (W. R. McPhun, 1834), 45, https://archive.org/details/philosophysleep02macngoog/page/n54/mode/2up.

Statement 7: Lewis Carroll, *Alice's Adventures in Wonderland and Through the Looking-Glass* (Modern Library, 2002), 162.

Statement 8: Gallagher Flinn, "How Mirrors Work," sec. 4 "Mirrors in Literature and Superstition," *How Stuff Works* (Aug. 5, 2009), https://science.howstuffworks.com/innovation/everyday-innovations/mirror4.htm.

Statement 12: Jennifer Nix, "Finding Poetry in Illness," *Poetry Foundation* (May 9, 2012), https://www.poetryfoundation.org/articles/69804/finding-poetry-in-illness.

Statement 15: Flinn, "How Mirrors Work," sec. 4.

Statements 18–19: John Berger, *Ways of Seeing* (Penguin, 1977), 47–51.

Statement 21: Jorge Luis Borges, *The Book of Imaginary Beings*, trans. Andrew Hurley (Penguin, 2006), 18–19.

Statement 22: Shakespeare, *Hamlet*, act 2, sc 2.

Statement 27: S. Y. Edgerton, "Brunelleschi's Mirror, Alberti's Window, and Galileo's 'Perspective Tube,'" *História, Ciências, Saúde-Manguinhos*, vol. 13 sup. (Oct. 2006): 151–79, https://doi.org/10.1590/ S0104-59702006000500010.

Statement 29: Hans Holbein the Younger, The Ambassadors, 1533, oil on oak, 207 × 209.5 cm, The National Gallery, London, https://www.nationalgallery.org.uk/paintings/ hans-holbein-the-younger-the-ambassadors.

Statements 30–31: "Mirror Test," *Wikipedia*, https:// en.wikipedia.org/wiki/Mirror_test; Chelsea Wald, "What Do Animals Think They See When They Look in a Mirror?," *Slate* (Oct. 24, 2014), https://slate.com/ technology/2014/10/what-do-animals-see-in-the- mirror-self-recognition-and-social-behavior-video. html. For an interesting take on the cultural limitations of the mirror test, see Maggie Koerth-Baker, "Kids (and Animals) Who Fail Classic Mirror Tests May Still Have Sense of Self," *Scientific American* (Nov. 29, 2010), https://www.scientificamerican.com/article/ kids-and-animals-who-fail-classic-mirror/.

Statement 32: "Rokeby Venus," *Wikipedia*, https:// en.wikipedia.org/wiki/Rokeby_Venus; Diego Velázquez, *The Toilet of Venus (The Rokeby Venus)*, 1647–51, oil on canvas, 122.5 × 177 cm, The National Gallery, London, http://www.nationalgallery.org.uk/paintings/ diego-velazquez-the-toilet-of-venus-the-rokeby-venus.

Statement 34: Natalie Angier, "Pigs Prove to Be Smart, If Not Vain," *The New York Times* (Nov. 9, 2009), https:// www.nytimes.com/2009/11/10/science/10angier.html.

Statement 35: Velázquez, *The Toilet of Venus*; Marco Bertamini, Richard Latto, and Alice Spooner, "The Venus Effect: People's Understanding of Mirror Reflections in Paintings," *Perception*, vol. 32, no. 5 (2003): 593– 599, https://www.bertamini.org/lab/Publications/ BertaminiLattoSpooner2003.pdf.

Statement 36: Diego Velázquez, *Las Meninas*, 1656, oil on canvas, 320.5 x 281.5 cm, Museo del Prado, Madrid, https://www.museodelprado.es/en/the-collection/art -work/las-meninas/9fdc7800-9ade-48b0-ab8b -edee94ea877f.

Statements 37–38: Velázquez, *The Toilet of Venus*; Philip McCouat, "From the Rokeby Venus to Fascism, Pt 1: Why Did Suffragettes Attack Artworks?," *Journal of Art in Society*, https://www.artinsociety.com/ from-the-rokeby-venus-to-fascism-pt-1-why-did- suffragettes-attack-artworks.html.

Statement 38: Of course, the suffragette in question later went on to become head of the women's section of

Oswald Mosley's British Union of Fascists. While she may not have been a slavering maniac, she was certainly capable of bad reasoning. McCouat, "From the Rokeby Venus to Fascism, Pt 2: The Strange Allure of Fascism," *Journal of Art in Society*, https://www.artinsociety.com/from-the-rokeby-venus-to-fascism-pt-2-the-strange-allure-of-fascism.html.

Statement 40: Ben Thomas, "What's So Special about Mirror Neurons?," *Scientific American* (Nov. 6, 2012), https://blogs.scientificamerican.com/guest-blog/whats-so-special-about-mirror-neurons/.

Statement 41: Christian Jarrett, "A Calm Look at the Most Hyped Concept in Neuroscience—Mirror Neurons," *Wired* (Dec. 13, 2013), https://www.wired.com/2013/12/a-calm-look-at-the-most-hyped-concept-in-neuroscience-mirror-neurons/.

Statement 42: Alfred Gottlieb and Mark Rothko, letter to Edward Aldin Jewell (Jun. 7, 1943), https://www.gottliebfoundation.org/blog/2021/9/28/from-the-archives-the-jewell-letters-theres-no-such-thing-as-good-painting-about-nothing; René Magritte, *The Treachery of Images (La Trahison des Images)*, 1929, oil on canvas, 23.75 × 31.94 inches, Los Angeles County Museum of Art, Los Angeles, https://collections.lacma.org/node/239578.

Statement 43: Pliny the Elder, *Natural History*, trans. John Bostock, bk. 35, ch. 36, http://data.perseus.org/

citations/urn:cts:latinLit:phi0978.phi001.perseus-eng1:35.36.

Statement 44: Jacques Lacan, *The Four Fundamental Concepts of Psychoanalysis*, ed. Jacques-Alain Miller, trans. Alan Sheridan (W. W. Norton, 1998), 103 and 112.

Statement 45: Catherine Belsey, "Love as Trompe-l'Oeil: Taxonomies of Desire in *Venus and Adonis*," *Shakespeare Quarterly*, vol. 46, no. 3 (Fall 1995): 257, https://doi.org/10.2307/2871118.

Statement 47: While the quotation is widely attributed to Wright, I have not been able to trace it conclusively. For an example of the attribution, see Gary Rolfe, *The University in Dissent: Scholarship in the Corporate University* (Routledge, 2013), 5.

Statement 48: Shakespeare, *Hamlet*, act 3, sc. 2; Oscar Wilde, *The Picture of Dorian Gray* (Canterbury Classics, 2013), v.

Statement 50: Mrinali Patel Gupta, "Acute Zonal Occult Outer Retinopathy," *VisionAware.org*, https://www.visionaware.org/info/your-eye-condition/guide-to-eye-conditions/azoor/; J. Donald M. Gass, "Acute zonal occult outer retinopathy," *Journal of Clinical Neuro-ophthalmology*, vol. 13, no. 2 (1993): 79–97, https://collections.lib.utah.edu/ark:/87278/s6k96dm6/225857.

Statement 56: T. S. Eliot, "Tradition and the Individual Talent" in *The Sacred Wood*, sec. 2, https://www.bartleby.com/200/sw4.html.

Statement 59: Anna Fels, "Great Betrayals," *The New York Times* (Oct. 5, 2013), https://www.nytimes.com/2013/10/06/opinion/sunday/great-betrayals.html.

Statement 61: Anne Bradstreet, "The Author to Her Book," *Poets.org*, https://www.poets.org/poem/author-her-book.

Statement 64: While this statement is widely attributed to Hurston, I have not been able to trace it conclusively. For an example of the attribution, see Mary Karr, *The Art of Memoir* (Harper, 2015), 27.

Meet Aristotle

Statement 2: Davis is in fact misquoting Gerald Edelman paraphrasing James. Jordan Davis, "Obscure Poetry in the Age of Google," *The Best American Poetry* (Feb. 12, 2012), https://blog.bestamericanpoetry.com/the_best_american_poetry/2012/02/obscure-poetry-in-the-age-of-google-by-jordan-davis.html; Gerald Edelman, *Second Nature: Brain Science and Human Knowledge* (Yale, 2006), 4; William James, "Does 'Consciousness' Exist?," *The Journal of Philosophy, Psychology and Scientific Methods*, vol. 1., no. 18 (Sep. 1, 1904): 478, https://archive.org/details/jstor-2011942/page/n1/mode/2up.

Statement 3: Christopher Shields, "Aristotle," *The Stanford Encyclopedia of Philosophy*, ed. Edward N. Zalta (Spring 2022), https://plato.stanford.edu/archives/spr2022/entries/aristotle/; "Aristotle," *History*, https://www.history.com/topics/ancient-history/aristotle; Wilhelm Windelband, *A History of Philosophy; With Especial Reference to the Formulation and Development of Its Problems and Conceptions*, trans. James Hayden Tufts (The MacMillan Co., 1914), 103–104, https://archive.org/details/windelbandsphilo00winduoft/page/102/mode/2up.

Statement 4: Oscar Wilde, *The Picture of Dorian Gray* (Canterbury Classics, 2013), v.

Statement 5: Philip Roth, as interviewed by Hermione Lee, "Philip Roth, The Art of Fiction, No. 84," *The Paris Review* (Fall 1984), https://www.theparisreview.org/interviews/2957/the-art-of-fiction-no-84-philip-roth.

Statement 6: Richard Feynman, "Cargo Cult Science" (1974), http://calteches.library.caltech.edu/51/2/CargoCult.htm.

Statement 7: Aristotle, *De Partibus Animalium*, trans. William Ogle, (Oxford, 1911), 676a, n.1, https://archive.org/details/b29012284/page/n141/mode/2up; Aristotle, *On the Parts of Animals, Parts I–IV*, trans. James G. Lennox (Clarendon Press, 2002), 285, commentary on 676^a3–5.

Statement 8: Christopher Shields, "Notes to Aristotle," *The Stanford Encyclopedia of Philosophy*, ed. Edward N. Zalta (Spring 2022), https://plato.stanford.edu/archives/spr2022/entries/aristotle/notes.html#3.

Statements 11, 13: Louis F. Groarke, "Aristotle: Logic," sec. 11, *Internet Encyclopedia of Philosophy*, https://iep.utm.edu/aristotle-logic/#H11.

Statement 14: Christopher Shields, "Notes to Aristotle."

Statement 18: Arthur Schopenhauer, *The World as Will and Idea (Vol. II)*, trans. R. B. Haldane and J. Kemp (Kegan Paul, Trench, Trübner & Co., 1909), 446, https://www.gutenberg.org/files/40097/40097-pdf.pdf.

Statement 22: kari edwards, "Narrative/Identity," *Narrativity*, no. 3 (May 2003), https://web.archive.org/web/20120110042824/http://www.sfsu.edu:80/~poetry/narrativity/issue_three/edwards.html.

Statement 23: While the quotation is widely attributed to Einstein, I have not been able to trace it conclusively. For an example of the attribution, see Sharon Guynup, "Is Seeing Believing?," *Scientific American* (Sep. 12, 2013), https://doi.org/10.1038/scientificamericanillusions0913-1; Feynman, "Cargo Cult Science."

A Good Attitude

Statement 2: Cal Bedient, "Against Conceptualism," *Boston Review* (Jul. 24, 2013), https://www.bostonreview.net/articles/against-conceptualism/.

Statement 5: Rosamond Kent Sprague, "Aristotle on Red Mirrors (On Dreams II 459b24-460a23)" *Phronesis,* vol. 30, no. 3 (1985): 323–325, http://www.jstor.org/stable/4182237.

Statement 9: James Longenbach, "A Fine Excess," *The Virtues of Poetry* (Graywolf, 2013), 79.

Statement 11: Kate Zambreno, *Frances Farmer Is My Sister,* (Jul. 3, 2013), https://web.archive.org/web/20130823190444/http://francesfarmerismysister.blogspot.com/.

Statement 12: Andrew Marvell, "To His Coy Mistress," *Poetry Foundation,* https://www.poetryfoundation.org/poems/44688/to-his-coy-mistress.

Statement 13: "The Boston Pill Trials," *PBS.org,* https://www.pbs.org/wgbh/americanexperience/features/pill-boston-pill-trials/; "Why Do I Menstruate While on Birth Control," *Go Ask Alice,* https://goaskalice.columbia.edu/answered-questions/why-do-i-menstruate-while-birth-control; Jonathan Eig, "The Team That Invented the Birth-Control Pill," *The Atlantic* (Oct. 9, 2014), http://www.theatlantic.com/health/archive/2014/10/ the-team-that-invented-the-birth-control-pill/380684/.

Statement 17: Craig Foltz, "Rich Girls Will Break Your Heart," *Diagram*, no. 12.3, http://thediagram.com/12_3/ foltz.html.

Statement 21: *The Kids in the Hall*, season 1, episode 4, dirs. Jack Budgell and Robert Boyd, written by David Foley, Bruce McCullough, Kevin McDonald, Mark McKinney, and Scott Thompson (Nov. 14, 1989).

Confessions of a Pareidoliac

Statement 3: "Pareidolia: Why We See Faces in Hills, the Moon and Toasties," *BBC Magazine* (May 13, 2013), https://www.bbc.com/news/magazine-22686500; Leonardo da Vinci, *A Treatise on Painting*, trans. John Francis Rigaud, Esq. (J. Taylor, 1802), ch CLXIII, https://www.gutenberg.org/cache/epub/46915/ pg46915-images.html#Chap_CLXIII); Franklin R. and Mary Ann Rogers, *Painting and Poetry: Form, Metaphor, and the Language of Literature* (Associated University Presses, 1985), 24.

Statement 4: Abigail Tucker, "Arcimboldo's Feast for the Eyes," *Smithsonian* (Jan. 2011), https://www.smithsonianmag .com/arts-culture/arcimboldos-feast-for-the-eyes -74732989/.

Statement 6: Stephanie Burt, "'LIKE' A speculative essay about poetry, simile, artificial intelligence, mourning, sex, rock and roll, grammar, romantic love," *American Poetry Review*, vol. 43, no. 1 (Jan./Feb. 2014), https://aprweb.org/poems/like-a-speculative-essay-about-poetry-simile-artificial-intelligence-mourning-sex-rock-and-roll-grammar-romantic-love.

Statement 7: *Brancusi v. United States*, 54 Treas. Dec. 428 (Customs Ct. 1928); Stéphanie Giry, "An Odd Bird," *Legal Affairs* (Sep./Oct. 2002), https://www.legalaffairs.org/issues/September-October-2002/story_giry_sepoct2002.msp.

Statement 9: Homer, *The Odyssey*, trans. A. T. Murray (Harvard, 1919), bk. 19, 277, https://www.loebclassics.com/view/homer-odyssey/1919/pb_LCL105.277.xml.

Statement 10: Naomi Epel, *Writers Dreaming: Twenty-Six Writers Talk About Their Dreams and the Creative Process* (Vintage, 1994), 55–58. Richard Ford was particularly hostile to the idea that his creative work had anything to do with dreaming.

Statement 12: Mark Strand, as interviewed by Wallace Shawn, "Mark Strand, The Art of Poetry, No. 77," *The Paris Review*, no. 148 (Fall 1998), https://www.theparisreview.org/interviews/1070/the-art-of-poetry-no-77-mark-strand.

Statement 15: Robert Trivers, *The Folly of Fools: The Logic of Deceit and Self-Deception in Human Life* (Basic Books, 2013), 23–24.

Statement 16: Aristotle, *On Dreams*, trans. J. I. Beare, http://classics.mit.edu/Aristotle/dreams.html; Synesius of Cyrene, *On Dreams*, trans. Isaac Myer (1888), 20–21, https://archive.org/details/ondreams00synegoog/page/n27/mode/2up.

Statement 17: Synesius of Cyrene, *On Dreams*, 30–33.

Statement 18: Christopher Benfey, "Tarot Dreams," *New York Review of Books* (Mar. 26, 2015), https://www.nybooks.com/daily/2015/03/26/tarot-dreams/.

Statement 22: Plato, *The Republic*, trans. Benjamin Jowett, bk. X, http://classics.mit.edu/Plato/republic.11.x.html; William Chase Greene, "Plato's View of Poetry," *Harvard Studies in Classical Philology*, vol. 29 (1918), 1, https://archive.org/details/jstor-310558/page/n1/mode/2up.

Statement 25: Raymond Tallis, "Notes Towards a Philosophy of Sleep," *Philosophy Now*, no. 91 (2012), https://philosophynow.org/issues/91/Notes_Towards_a_Philosophy_of_Sleep; Aristotle, *On Dreams*.

Statement 26: Fyodor Dostoevsky, "The Dream of a Queer Fellow," in *Pages from the Journal of an Author*, trans. S. Koteliansky & J. Middleton Murry (John W. Luce

and Co., 1916), 13, https://archive.org/details/
pagesfromjourna00murrgoog/page/n29/mode/2up.

Statements 31–33: Maclen Stanley, "Monsters in the
Mirror: No Really, Literal Monsters," *Psychology
Today* (Aug. 2, 2014), https://www.psychologytoday.
com/us/blog/making-sense-chaos/201408/
monsters-in-the-mirror-no-really-literal-monsters.

Statement 34: Jessica Smith (@thedaybooks), 1:02 a.m.
(Jun. 9, 2015), https://twitter.com/thedaybooks/
status/608137158436749312.

Statement 36: Deborah Cameron, "What Language
Barrier?," *The Guardian* (Oct. 1, 2007), https://www.
theguardian.com/world/2007/oct/01/gender.books.

Statement 39: Katha Politt, "Foreword," in Carolyn G.
Heilbrun, *Writing A Woman's Life* (W. W. Norton, 1988), xvi.

Statement 45: Aristotle, *On Dreams*.

Statement 48: Sylvia Plath, "Mirror," *All Poetry*, https://
allpoetry.com/poem/8498499-Mirror-by-Sylvia-Plath.

Statement 51: Christina DeBusk, "Feng Shui Tips for
Your Bedroom," in "Using Feng Shui for Your Mental
Health," *Verywell Mind*, https://www.verywellmind.com/
feng-shui-tips-for-your-bedroom-88934.

Statements 55–56: Tim Wilkinson, "Mirror, Mirror," *Philosophy Now*, no. 114 (Jun./Jul. 2016), https://philosophynow.org/issues/114/Mirror_Mirror; Robbie Gonzalez, "Why do mirrors reverse left and right, but not top and bottom?," *Gizmodo* (Dec. 26, 2012), https://gizmodo.com/why-do-mirrors-reverse-left-and-right-but-not-top-and-5971306.

Statements 57–58: "Claude Monet's Poppies, Near Argenteuil," *Color Vision & Art*, https://www.webexhibits.org/colorart/monet2.html; "Luminance Differences Affect Our Perceptions," *Color Vision & Art*, https://www.webexhibits.org/colorart/anuszkiewicz.html.

Statement 61: Giry, "An Odd Bird."

Statements 62–63: Jorge Luis Borges, *Labyrinths: Selected Stories & Other Writings*, eds. Donald A. Yates and James E. Erby, (Modern Library, 1983), 246–47.

Statement 68: Rosalie Moore, "The Mind's Disguise," *The Grasshopper's Man* (Yale University Press, 1949), 13.

Statement 69: Vivian Gornick, *The Situation and the Story* (Farrar, Straus and Giroux, 2001), 23.

Statement 71: Quoted in Efraín Kristal, *Invisible work: Borges and Translation* (Vanderbilt University Press, 2002), 23–24.

Statement 75: W. B. Yeats, "The Tower," *Poets.org*, https://www.poets.org/poem/tower.

Statement 78: Robert Lowell, "The Poetry of John Berryman," *The New York Review of Books* (May 28, 1964), https://www.nybooks.com/articles/1964/05/28/the-poetry-of-john-berryman/.

Statement 80: *Brancusi v. United States*.

Statements 81, 83: Synesius of Cyrene, *On Dreams*, 25 and 5.

Statement 87: *Brancusi v. United States*.

Double-Paned

Statement 1: The "windows" version is an idiomatic phrase in English; the "mirror" one, in French.

Statement 3: *L'sang d'un poète*, dir. Jean Cocteau, (1930), film; Petre Petrov, "The Modernist Mirror and the Hold of Being: Rilke and Zamiatin," *Studies in 20th & 21st Century Literature*, vol. 34, no. 2, (2010): 233, https://doi.org/10.4148/2334-4415.1731.

Statement 7: Ethan Siegel, "Observing the Universe Really Does Change the Outcome, and This Experiment Shows How," *Forbes* (May 26, 2020), https://www.forbes.com/sites/startswithabang/2020/05/26/

observing-the-universe-really-does-change-the-outcome-and-this-experiment-shows-how/.

Statements 9–10: Joan Retallack, *The Poethical Wager* (University of California, 2004), 14 and 22.

Statement 12: "Argos Panoptes," *Wikipedia*, https://en.wikipedia.org/wiki/Argus_Panoptes; Ovid, *The Metamorphoses*, trans. Horace Gregory (Signet Classics, 2009), 22–25.

Statement 17: Apollodorus, *The Library (Book II)*, trans. J. G. Frazer, 2.4.2, https://www.theoi.com/Text/Apollodorus2.html#4.

Statement 18: Ovid, *The Metamorphoses*, trans. Horace Gregory (Signet Classics, 2009), 65–69.

Statement 19: Rudine Sims Bishop, "Mirrors, Windows, and Sliding Glass Doors," *Perspectives: Choosing and Using Books for the Classroom*, vol. 6, no. 3 (Summer 1990), https://scenicregional.org/wp-content/uploads/2017/08/Mirrors-Windows-and-Sliding-Glass-Doors.pdf.

Statement 23: Michel Foucault, *Discipline and Punish: The Birth of the Prison*, trans. Alan Sheridan (Vintage, 1995), 200.

The (Only) Good Fascist

Statement 2: At least, there's no necessary distinction to be made, given that a fundamental aspect of totalitarianism is its need to rely on foundational myths, which are expounded and amplified by poets. Slavoj Žižek, "The Poetic Torture-House of Language: How Poetry Relates to Ethnic Cleansing," *Poetry* (Mar. 2014), https://www.poetryfoundation.org/poetrymagazine/articles/70096/the-poetic-torture-house-of-language; Slavoj Žižek, "Against Aristocratic Pride: Shakespeare and Radical Politics" (Apr. 9, 2013), *The Australian Broadcasting Corporation*, https://www.abc.net.au/religion/against-aristocratic-pride-shakespeare-and-radical-politics/10099914 (where he remarks "There is no ethnic cleansing without poetry."); Slavoj Žižek, "The Military-Poetic Complex," *London Review of Books*, vol. 30, no. 16 (Aug. 14, 2008), https://www.lrb.co.uk/the-paper/v30/n16/slavoj-zizek/the-military-poetic-complex; Slavoj Žižek, "Underground, or Ethnic Cleansing as a Continuation of Poetry by Other Means," *InterCommunication*, vol. 18 (Autumn 1996), http://www.ntticc.or.jp/pub/ic_mag/ic018/intercity/zizek_E.html.

Statement 3: Anthony Madrid, "If I Am a Total Washout as a Lover (And I Am)," in *I Am Your Slave Now Do What I Say* (Canarium, 2012), 89.

Statement 5: Ben Lerner, *The Hatred of Poetry* (Farrar, Straus and Giroux, 2016), 65.

Statement 6: John Metta, "I, Racist," *The Huffington Post* (Jul. 10, 2015), https://www.huffpost.com/entry/i-racist_b_7770652.

Statement 8: Richard Hugo, *The Triggering Town* (W. W. Norton & Co., 1979), 61.

Statement 9: See the 45th President of the United States.

Statement 13: Roderick T. Long, "Thinking Our Anger," talk transcript (Oct. 5, 2001), https://praxeology.net/libertariannation/a/n03012. Of course, as Long goes on explain, Aristotle also tried to bootstrap this idea into a justification for enslaving people.

Statement 14: Carolyn G. Heilbrun, *Writing A Woman's Life* (W. W. Norton, 1988), 15.

Statement 15: Claudia Rankine, *Citizen: An American Lyric* (Graywolf, 2014); Katy Waldman, "The New Printing of *Citizen* Adds a Haunting Message About Police Brutality," *Slate* (Jan. 7, 2015), https://slate.com/culture/2015/01/claudia-rankines-citizen-new-printing-mourns-michael-brown-eric-garner-black-victims-of-police-brutality.html.

Statement 16: *Broom: An International Magazine of the Arts*, vol. 4, no. 2 (Jan. 1923): 138, https://bluemountain.princeton.edu/bluemtn/?a=d&d=bmtnaap192301-01&e=-------en-20--1--txt-txIN-------. The reviewer is identified in the issue's table of contents only as "M. J.," but is likely *Broom*'s associate editor, Matthew Josephson.

Statement 18: Morgan Parker, "A Brief History of the Present," *Literary Hub* (Aug. 11, 2015), http://lithub.com/a-brief-history-of-the-present/.

Statement 21: Archibald MacLeish, *Poetry and Opinion* (University of Illinois, 1950), 41–42.

Statement 22: Ariana Reines, untitled blog post (Jan. 10, 2014), https://arianareines.tumblr.com/post/72901595108/i-loved-his-rage-and-rage-is-a-danger-to.

Statement 24: As quoted in Carolyn G. Heilbrun, *Writing A Woman's Life*, 71.

Statement 26: Ariana Reines, (Jan. 10, 2014).

Statement 27: Lyn Heijinian, "The Rejection of Closure," *Poetry Foundation*, (Oct. 13, 2009), https://www.poetryfoundation.org/articles/69401/the-rejection-of-closure.

Statement 28: Mark Strand, as interviewed by Wallace Shawn, "Mark Strand, The Art of Poetry, No. 77," *The Paris Review*, no. 148 (Fall 1998), https://www.theparisreview.org/interviews/1070/the-art-of-poetry-no-77-mark-strand.

Statement 29: Wendell Berry, "Notes: Unspecializing Poetry," in *Standing by Words: Essays* (North Point Press, 1983), 86.

Statement 33: John 14:27 (New American Standard Bible).

Statement 35: Bertolt Brecht, "Writing the Truth: Five Difficulties" in *Galileo*, trans. Charles Laughton (Grove Press, 1966),148.

Statement 36: John 18:38 (New International Version).

Statement 37: Richard Janko, "Aristotle on the Purpose of Literature," in Aristotle, *Poetics*, trans. Richard Janko (Hackett Pub, 1987), xvi–xx; Hans-Georg Gadamer, *Truth and Method*, trans. Joel Weinsheimer and Donald G. Marshall (Bloomsbury 2013), 133.

Statement 38: Sir Ian McKellen, as interviewed by Marc Maron, *WTF with Marc Maron* (podcast), ep. 621 (Jul. 20, 2015), http://www.wtfpod.com/podcast/episodes/episode_621_-_sir_ian_mckellen.

Statement 39: Johanna Hedva, "Sick Woman Theory," (Mar. 2015), https://topicalcream.org/features/sick-woman-theory/.

Tone Police

Statement 1: "Miranda Warning," *Legal Information Institute*, https://www.law.cornell.edu/wex/miranda_warning;

"Miranda Rights," *History* (Jun. 23, 2022), https://www.history.com/topics/united-states-constitution/miranda-rights.

Statement 5: "Appeal to Authority," *Logically Fallacious*, https://www.logicallyfallacious.com/logicalfallacies/Appeal-to-Authority.

Statement 6: Olivia Laing, "The future of loneliness," *The Guardian* (Apr. 1, 2015), http://www.theguardian.com/society/2015/apr/01/future-of-loneliness-internet-isolation.

Statement 8: Possidius, *Sancti Augustini Vita*, ed. Herbert T. Weiskotten (Princeton University Press, 1919), 142–143, https://archive.org/details/sanctiaugustiniv00possrich/page/142/mode/2up. The original Latin is "Quod legis ecce loquor, vox tua nempe mea est." at 142. Weiskotten provides a very flowery English version: "These words thou readest, lo, I speak! Thy voice is but my breath." at 143. I've opted for something a little less decorative.

Statement 9: Michelle Detorie (@mdetorie), 10:05 p.m. (Dec. 18, 2014), https://twitter.com/mdetorie/status/545776958861082624.

Statement 10: Maggie Balistreri, *The Evasion-English Dictionary* (Melville House, 2003), 66.

Statement 13: James Baldwin, "Florida Forum," WCKT-Miami, interview (Jun. 28, 1963), 17:45, https://youtu.be/FpRziHGxeEU?t=1063.

Statement 14: Because I am a total nerd, my first exposure to this Britishism was *Monty Python and the Holy Grail* (film, dirs. Terry Gilliam and Terry Jones, 1975), in which it's said by the alleged witch that John Cleese accuses of turning him into a newt.

Statement 15: Audre Lorde, "The Uses of Anger: Women Responding to Racism," *Sister, Outsider: Essays and Speeches* (Crossing Press, 2007), 128.

Statement 17: Robert Trivers, *The Folly of Fools: The Logic of Deceit and Self-Deception in Human Life* (Basic Books, 2013), 14.

Statement 18: Tim Parks, "A Weapon for Readers," *The New York Review of Books* (Dec. 3, 2014), https://www.nybooks.com/online/2014/12/03/weapon-for-readers/.

Statement 19: Alice Notley, *Dr. Williams' Heiresses, Tuumba*, vol. 28, (Tuumba Press, 1980), 16 (or 10 in pdf below), http://eclipsearchive.org/projects/TUUMBA/TUUMBA28/Tuumba28.pdf.

Statement 22: Sueyeun Juliette Lee, review of Bhanu Khapil's "Ban en Banlieue," *The Constant Critic*

(Jun. 7, 2015), http://www.constantcritic.com/
sueyeun_juliette_lee/ban-en-banlieue/.

Statement 23: Laurie Penny, "On Nerd Entitlement,"
The New Statesman (Dec. 29, 2014), https://
www.newstatesman.com/society/2014/12/
on-nerd-entitlement-rebel-alliance-empire.

Statement 24: Maxine Greene, "Curriculum and
Consciousness," *Teachers College Record*, vol. 73, no. 2
(1971), 253–70, https://maxinegreene.org/uploads/
library/curriculum_consciousness.pdf.

Statement 26: Richard Hugo, *The Triggering Town* (W. W.
Norton & Co., 1979), 7.

Statement 30: Vivian Gornick, *The Situation and the Story*
(Farrar, Straus and Giroux, 2001), 141–142.

Statement 31: Claudia Rankine, *Don't Let Me Be Lonely*
(Graywolf, 2004).

Statement 33: This phrase has become something of a trope.
The first instance I am aware of is Nathan Lane's character
saying it in *The Birdcage* (film, dir. Mike Nichols, 1996).

Statement 35: Christopher Nealon, "Heteronomy,"
Heteronomy (Edge Books, 2014), 62.

Statement 36: Pema Chödrön, *Start Where You Are* (Shambhala, 1994), 73.

Statement 38: Audre Lorde, "Poetry Is Not a Luxury," *Sister, Outsider*, 36.

Statement 40: Simone de Beauvoir, *All Said and Done* (Paragon House, 1994), 16.

Statement 44: The quotation is widely attributed to Moses ben Mamon, commonly known as Maimonides, but I have not been able to trace it conclusively. For an example of the attribution, the American artist Ben Shahn painted a portrait of Maimonides in 1954 that features the quote: "Maimonides" (1954), tempera on paper mounted on panel, 35.5 x 26.5 inches, Jewish Museum, New York, https://thejewishmuseum.org/collection/28120-maimonides.

Statement 45: Joan Retallack, *The Poethical Wager* (University of California, 2004), 23.

Statement 46: Dawn Lundy Martin, "Three Questions with Dawn Lundy Martin," interview by Danniel Schoonebeek, *PEN America Blog* (Sep. 23, 2015), https://pen.org/three-questions-with-dawn-lundy-martin/.

Statement 48: Maxine Greene, "Curriculum and Consciousness," 253–270.

Statement 49: Audre Lorde, "Learning from the 60s," *Sister, Outsider*, 141–142.

His Masterpiece

Statements 2–3: Justin Erik Halldór Smith, "Phyllis Rides Aristotle," (Apr. 2, 2013), https://www.jehsmith.com/1/2013/04/phyllis-rides-aristotle.html; "Aquamanile in the Form of Aristotle and Phyllis" (late 14th or early 15th century), bronze and quaternary copper alloy, 32.5 cm x 17.9 cm, The Metropolitan Museum of Art, New York, https://www.metmuseum.org/art/collection/search/459202; "Study and Love: Aristotle's Fall," *The Virtual Museum of Education Iconics*, University of Minnesota, https://iconics.cehd.umn.edu/Aristotle/Lecture/default.html.

Statement 4: It wasn't Season 9's infamous episode 16, "The First Time," in which Natalie has sex with her boyfriend, Snake, and then he doesn't call the next day and everyone thinks she's a slut. It was Season 8, episode 3 ("Ready or Not"), in which Tootie starts to get "serious" with her boyfriend Rudy, but won't accept advice from Beverly about it.

Statement 6: Iris Murdoch, "The Idea of Perfection," in *The Sovereignty of Good* (Schocken, 1971), 34.

Statement 8: Aristotle, *Generation of Animals*, trans. A. L. Peck (Harvard University Press, 1943), 5, https://

archive.org/details/generationofanim00arisuoft/page/4/mode/2up; F. Gonzalez-Crussi, "Generation: Past, Present, and Future," *Three Forms of Sudden Death: And Other Reflections on the Grandeur and Misery of the Body* (Picador, 1987), 3–4. Aristotle does appear to have thought that some insects, at least, arose from "putrescent matter." Aristotle, *Generation of Animals*, 7, https://archive.org/details/generationofanim00arisuoft/page/6/mode/2up.

Statement 9: F. Gonzalez-Crussi, *Three Forms of Sudden Death*, 3–4.

Statement 10: Amherst Manuscript #372, *Emily Dickinson Archive*, https://www.edickinson.org/editions/1/image_sets/12177283.

Statement 12: Raymond S. Nickerson, "Confirmation Bias: A Ubiquitous Phenomenon in Many Guises," *Review of General Psychology*, vol. 2, no. 2 (1998): 175–220, https://pages.ucsd.edu/~mckenzie/nickersonConfirmationBias.pdf.

Statements 13–14: Pseudo-Aristotle, *Aristotle's Works: The Master-Piece* (1900), https://archive.org/details/b2901248x; Mary Fissell, "When the Birds and the Bees Were Not Enough: Aristotle's Masterpiece," *Public Domain Review* (Aug. 19, 2015), https://publicdomainreview.org/essay/when-the-birds-and-the-bees-were-not-enough-aristotle-s-masterpiece/.

Statement 17: Mary E. Fissell, "Hairy Women and Naked Truths: Gender and the Politics of Knowledge in Aristotle's Masterpiece," *The William and Mary Quarterly*, vol. 60, no. 1 (2003): 43 and 49, https://doi.org/10.2307/3491495.

Statement 19: Wallace Stevens, *The Necessary Angel: Essays on Reality and the Imagination* (Vintage, 1951), 33.

Statement 20: Ann Friedman, "Astronaut Sally Ride and the Burden of Being the First," *The American Prospect* (Jun. 19, 2014), https://prospect.org/culture/books/astronaut-sally-ride-burden-first/.

Statement 23: Julia C. Obert, "What we talk about when we talk about intimacy," *Emotion, Space and Society*, vol. 21 (Nov. 2016): 25 and 28–29, https://doi.org/10.1016/j.emospa.2016.10.002.

Statement 25: "Study and Love: Aristotle's Fall," *The Virtual Museum of Education Iconics*.

Metaphor as Illness

Statement 1: I am indebted to Anne Boyer's "All the Gold in California" (Nov. 8, 2013) and its discussion of events versus conditions, for permitting me to make this connection. A pdf can be found at https://docs.google.com/file/d/0B0NSr5BoYUEIb19UeDBUNS1ZcWM/edit?resourcekey=0-EH6o2iO8Pv50DFbAoHbPJA.

Statement 6: For an example of an Amsler grid, see Kierstan Boyd, "Have AMD? Save Your Sight with an Amsler Grid," *AMD.org* (May 26, 2020), https://www.aao.org/eye-health/tips-prevention/facts-about-amsler-grid-daily-vision-test.

Statement 8: Susan Sontag, *Illness as Metaphor* (Farrar, Straus and Giroux, 1978), 40.

Statement 10: Virginia Woolf, "On Being Ill," *The New Criterion*, vol. 4, no. 1 (Jan. 1926): 32, https://thenewcriterion1926.files.wordpress.com/2014/12/woolf-on-being-ill.pdf.

Statement 11: Anne Boyer, "All the Gold in California."

Statement 12: David M. Jackson, "Bach, Handel, and the Chevalier Taylor," *Medical History*, vol. 12, no. 4 (Oct. 1968): 385–393, https://www.ncbi.nlm.nih.gov/pmc/articles/PMC1033864/pdf/medhist00141-0072.pdf; "Handel, Bach were Blinded by '18th Century Quackery,'" *University of Wisconsin-Madison School of Medicine and Public Health* (Dec. 14, 2009), https://www.med.wisc.edu/news-and-events/2009/december/handel-bach-blinded-18th-century-quackery/.

Statement 13: John Taylor, *Records of My Life* (J & J Harper 1833), 25, https://www.google.com/books/edition/Records_of_My_Life/SzlDAAAAIAAJ?hl=en.

Statements 14–15: Wallace Stevens, "From Miscellaneous Notebooks," *Opus Posthumous* (Vintage, 1989), 204. Specifically, Stevens says that "Reality is a cliché / From which we escape by metaphor."

Statement 16: J. Donald Gass, Anita Agarwal, and Ingrid U. Scott, "Acute Zonal Occult Outer Retinopathy: A Long-Term Follow-Up Study," *American Journal of Ophthalmology*, vol. 134, no. 3 (Sep. 2002): 329–339 , https://doi.org/10.1016/s0002-9394(02)01640-9.

Statement 18: *The Oxford English Dictionary* (2d ed. Oxford University Press 1991), vol. 9, 676.

Statement 19: Max Black, "Metaphor," *Proceedings of the Aristotelian Society*, New Series, vol. 55 (1954–1955): 281, https://web.stanford.edu/~eckert/PDF/Black1954.pdf.

Statement 26: George Lakoff & Mark Johnson, *Metaphors We Live By* (University of Chicago Press, 2003), 4–6.

Statement 32: Susan Sontag, *Illness as Metaphor*, 21–23.

Statement 38: Aristotle, *Rhetoric*, trans. W. Rhys Roberts, bk. 3, pt. 11, http://classics.mit.edu/Aristotle/rhetoric.3.iii.html.

Statement 41: Thomas Sprat, *The History of the Royal Society of London, For the Improving of Natural Knowledge* (London, 1667), 111–115, https://www.google.com

/books/edition/The_History_of_the_Royal_Society
_of_Lond/g30OAAAAQAAJ.

Statement 42: Letter from Lyn Heijinian to Charles Bernstein
(Dec. 6, 1986), reprinted in *Aerial 10: Lyn Heijinian*, eds.
Rod Smith & Jen Hofer (Aerial/Edge 2016), 98.

Statement 46: "The Grande Dame of Dance: A Book and
Show for Agnes de Mille," *Life* (Nov. 15, 1963): 94,
https://books.google.com/books?id=RlIEAAAAMBAJ
&lpg=PP1&pg=PA89#v=onepage&q&f=false.

Statement 49: Jacques Derrida, "White Mythology:
Metaphor in the Text of Philosophy," *New Literary
History*, vol. 6, no. 1, (Autumn 1974): 56, http://www.
vu.centrumethos.nl/wp-content/uploads/2017/05/
derrida-white-mythology.pdf.

Statement 50: I have no way of tracing the exact news article
my husband read, but for confirmation that this feat of
scientific freakiness took place, see David Noonan, "Meet
the Two Scientists Who Implanted a False Memory
Into a Mouse," *Smithsonian* (Nov. 2014), https://www.
smithsonianmag.com/innovation/meet-two-scientists-
who-implanted-false-memory-mouse-180953045/.

Statements 53–54: Virginia Woolf, "Professions for
Women," *The Death of the Moth, and Other Essays*,
https://gutenberg.net.au/ebooks12/1203811h.
html#ch-28.

Statements 55–57: Klaus Ziegler, "Ojo y visión; la triste historia de Sidney Bradford," *El Espectador* (Jul. 30, 2015), https://www.elespectador.com/opinion/columnistas/klaus-ziegler/ojo-y-vision-la-triste-historia-de-sidney-bradford-column-576178/; Richard Gregory and Jean Wallace, "Recovery from Early Blindness—A Case Study," http://www.richardgregory.org/papers/recovery_blind/recovery-from-early-blindness.pdf.

Statement 59: Variations on this phrase have become stock-in-trade for film and television vamps. The original version appears to be, "Would you be shocked if I put on something more comfortable?," spoken by Jean Harlow in the film *Hell's Angels*, directed by, all all people, Howard Hughes. Caryn James, "Critic's Notebook; A No-Apologies Woman for the 90's: Harlow," *The New York Times* (Oct. 1, 1993), C-1, https://www.nytimes.com/1993/10/01/movies/critic-s-notebook-a-no-apologies-woman-for-the-90-s-harlow.html.

Statement 60: Joanna Bourke, *The Story of Pain: From Prayer to Painkillers* (Oxford University Press, 2017), 87.

Statement 61: Martha King, "Outside Inside," *A Public Space*, no. 23 (2015): 170.

Statement 62: Jacques Derrida, *Memoirs of the Blind: The Self-Portrait and Other Ruins*, trans. Pascale-Anne Brault and Michael Naas (University of Chicago Press, 1993), 4.

Statement 63: Israel Shenker, "Borges, a Blind Writer with Insight," *The New York Times* (Apr. 6, 1971), https://www.nytimes.com/books/97/08/31/reviews/borges-insight.html; "John Milton," *Poets.org*, https://www.poets.org/poetsorg/poet/john-milton; Tom Jacobs, "Why Did Bach Go Blind?," *Pacific Standard* (Feb. 26, 2013), https://psmag.com/economics/why-did-bach-go-blind-53250; "Science Watch; Monet's Vision," *The New York Times* (Nov. 12, 1985), https://www.nytimes.com/1985/11/12/science/science-watch-monet-s-vision.html; "George Frideric Handel," *Biography.com* (Apr. 2, 2014), https://www.biography.com/musicians/george-handel; Peter G. Watson, "The Enigma of Galileo's Eyesight: Some Novel Observations on Galileo Galilei's Vision and His Progression to Blindness," *Survey of Ophthalmology*, vol. 54, no. 5 (Sep.–Oct. 2009): 630–40, https://doi.org/10.1016/j.survophthal.2009.03.002.

Statement 64: Guy Debord, *The Society of the Spectacle* (Bureau of Public Secrets, 2014), ch. 1, epigraph.

Statement 65: Jorge Luis Borges, *Professor Borges: A Course on English Literature* (New Directions, 2013, Kindle e-book ed.), Class 5 (Oct. 24, 1966). Borges attributes the idea to a "French composer from the last century," who said that "to express silence in music, I would need three military bands." This quotation appears, in the original French, in George Moore's memoir, *Confessions of a Young Man*, originally published in 1886, where it is attributed to Ernest Cabaner. George Moore, *Confessions of a Young Man*, ch. 8, https://www.gutenberg.org/files/12278/12278-h/12278-h.htm#VIII.

Statement 67: "James Joyce Dies; Wrote 'Ulysses,'" *The New York Times* (Jan. 13, 1941), https://archive.nytimes.com/www.nytimes.com/books/00/01/09/specials/joyce-obit.html; Anna Gruener, "Degas' 'Exercise of Circumvention,'" *British Journal of General Practice*, vol. 64, no. 622, (May 2014), https://doi.org/10.3399/bjgp14X679796.

Statement 68: Jacques Derrida, *Memoirs of the Blind*, 5.

Statement 73: Richard Cavendish, "Nelson's Victory at Copenhagen," *History Today*, vol. 61, no. 4 (Apr. 2011), https://www.historytoday.com/archive/nelsons-victory-copenhagen.

Statement 77: Variations on the phrase "call 'em like [I, you, or whoever] see 'em" are common currency. The phrase originates in a joke apparently first related in a scholarly article on the nature of perception. In brief, three umpires are discussing how they distinguish balls from strikes. The first umpire says "Some's balls and some's strikes and I calls 'em as they is." The second says that "Some's balls and some's strikes and I calls 'em as I sees 'em." The last umpire, with a Nelsonian flourish, says, "Some's balls and some's strikes, but they ain't nothin' till I calls 'em." Hadley Cantril, "Perception and Interpersonal Relations," *The American Journal of Psychiatry*, vol. 114, iss. 2 (Aug. 1957),

126, https://ajp.psychiatryonline.org/doi/abs/10.1176/ajp.114.2.119.

Dispatch from the Uncanny Valley

Statement 1: Charles William Eliot, *Addresses at the Inauguration of Charles William Eliot as President of Harvard College, Tuesday, Oct. 19, 1869* (Sever and Francis, 1869), 49–51, https://archive.org/details/addressesatinaug02harv/page/48/mode/2up.

Statement 2: Daniel J. Hemel, "Summers' Comments on Women and Science Draw Ire," *The Harvard Crimson* (Jan. 14, 2005), https://www.thecrimson.com/article/2005/1/14/summers-comments-on-women-and-science/.

Statements 7–8: Stephanie Lay, "Uncanny Valley: Why We Find Human-like Robots and Dolls So Creepy," *The Guardian* (Nov. 13, 2015), https://www.theguardian.com/commentisfree/2015/nov/13/robots-human-uncanny-valley.

Statement 12: Hari Ziyad, "Empathy Won't Save Us In the Fight Against Oppression. Here's Why.," *BGD* (Aug. 11, 2015), http://www.bgdblog.org/2015/08/empathy-wont-save-us-in-the-fight-against-oppression-heres-why/.

Statement 13: D. W. Winnicott, *Home Is Where We Start From: Essays by a Psychoanalyst* (W. W. Norton, 1990), 125.

Statement 14: "Paranoia knows some things well and others poorly." Eve Kosofsky Sedgwick, "Paranoid Reading and Reparative Reading, Or, You're So Paranoid, You Probably Think This Essay Is About You," in *Touching Feeling: Affect, Pedagogy, Performativity* (Duke University Press, 2002), 130.

Statement 18: Adam Phillips and Barbara Taylor, *On Kindness* (Penguin, 2010), 6.

Statement 24: For an example of the attribution, see Keld Jensen, "Control Is Good, But Trust Is Cheaper," *Forbes* (Dec. 8, 2014), https://www.forbes.com/sites /keldjensen/2014/12/08/control-is-good-trust-is -cheaper/#1c80b4611322.

Statement 26: Maureen Thorson, "The Worst That Could Happen," in *Share the Wealth* (Veliz Books, 2022), 65. Citing myself is ridiculous but I couldn't resist.

Statement 39: Catharine A. MacKinnon, "Privacy v. Equality: Beyond Roe v. Wade," in *Feminism Unmodified: Discourses on Life and Law* (Harvard University Press, 1987), 93–102.

Statements 43–46: Eve Kosofsky Sedgwick, in *Touching Feeling,* 130 and146.

Statements 51–53: Julia C. Obert, "What We Talk About When We Talk About Intimacy," in *Emotion, Space and*

Society, vol. 21 (2016): 25–32, https://doi.org/10.1016/j.
emospa.2016.10.002.

Statements 54–55: "Leta Stetter Hollingworth," *Wikipedia*,
https://en.m.wikipedia.org/wiki/Leta_Stetter_
Hollingworth; "Functional Periodicity," *Wikipedia*,
https://en.m.wikipedia.org/wiki/Functional_periodicity;
Leta Stetter Hollingworth, "Functional Periodicity: An
Experimental Study of the Mental and Motor Abilities
of Women During Menstruation," http://psychclassics.
yorku.ca/Hollingworth/Periodicity/.

Statement 57: Shawn Hamilton, "What Those Who
Studied Nazis Can Teach Us About the Strange
Reaction to Donald Trump," *The Huffington Post* (Dec.
19, 2016), https://www.huffpost.com/entry/donald-
trump-nazi-propaganda-coordinate_n_58583b6fe4b08d
ebb78a7d5c.

Statements 58–59: Lawrence H. Summers, "'Political
Correctness' Has Become a Codeword for Hate,"
The Washington Post (Nov. 17, 2016), https://www.
washingtonpost.com/news/wonk/wp/2016/11/17/
larry-summers-political-correctness-has-become-a-
codeword-for-hate/.

Statement 60: Erika Andersen, "Learning to Learn," *Harvard
Business Review* (Mar. 2016): 98–101, https://hbr.
org/2016/03/learning-to-learn.

Statement 62: *Ecclesiastes* 1:18 (King James Version).

Statement 66: Madeleine Davies, "Becoming Ugly," *Jezebel* (Dec. 29, 2016), http://jezebel.com/becoming-ugly-1789622154.

A Likely Story

Statement 1: T. S. Eliot, "Tradition and the Individual Talent" in *The Sacred Wood*, sec. 2, https://www.bartleby.com/200/sw4.html.

Statement 4: Oliver Sacks, "Speak, Memory," *The New York Review of Books* (Feb. 21, 2013), https://www.nybooks.com/articles/2013/02/21/speak-memory/.

Statement 5: Jessica Smith, "TtD Supplement #18: Seven Questions for Jessica Smith," *Touch the Donkey* (Feb. 3, 2015), http://touchthedonkey.blogspot.com/2015/02/ttd-supplement-18-seven-questions-for.html.

Statement 7: Francis A. Yates, *The Art of Memory* (Pimlico 2007, e-book ed.), ch. 2; Plato, *Phaedrus*, trans. Benjamin Jowett, http://classics.mit.edu/Plato/phaedrus.html (Socrates's tale of the Egyptian city of Naucratis).

Statement 13: Alfred, Lord Tennyson, "The Lady of Shalott," *Poetry Foundation*, https://www.poetryfoundation.org/poems/45359/the-lady-of-shalott-1832.

Statement 14: Maggie Nelson, *The Red Parts* (Graywolf, 2007), 155.

Statement 21: Sir Philip Sidney, *The Defense of Poesy*, https://www.bartleby.com/27/1.html.

Statement 23: Jacques Derrida, "'To Do Justice to Freud': The History of Madness in the Age of Psychoanalysis," trans. Pascale-Anne Brault and Michael Naas, *Critical Inquiry*, vol. 20, no. 2 (Winter 1994): 227, https://doi.org/10.1086/448710.

Statement 25: Jorge Luis Borges, "Cambridge." The text of the poem in the original Spanish may be found at https://www.poeticous.com/borges/cambridge.

Statement 26: Erika Hayasaki, "Traces of Times Lost," *The Atlantic* (Nov. 29, 2016), https://www.theatlantic.com/health/archive/2016/11/childhood-memory-amensia/508886/; Vlad Chituc, "Would You Rather Lose Your Morals or Your Memory?," *The New Republic* (Aug. 12, 2015), https://newrepublic.com/article/122516/would-you-rather-lose-your-morals-or-your-memory.

Statement 29: Jenny Offill, *Dept. of Speculation* (Knopf, 2014), 140.

Statement 30: Camille T. Dungy, "Notes from the Lower Level," *Guernica* (Jun. 16, 2017), https://www.guernicamag.com/notes-from-the-lower-level/.

Statements 32–33: Sigmund Freud, *The Interpretation of Dreams*, trans. A. A. Brill (Macmillan, 1913), 127, https://archive.org/details/in.ernet.dli.2015.854/page/n123/mode/2up.

Statement 35: Aleksandar Hemon, "Stop Making Sense, or How to Write in the Age of Trump," *The Village Voice* (Jan. 17, 2017), https://www.villagevoice.com/2017/01/17/stop-making-sense-or-how-to-write-in-the-age-of-trump/.

Statements 40–41: Brian Blanchfield, *Proxies: Essays Near Knowing* (Nightboat, 2016), throughout and vii.

Statement 42: John Keats, Letter to George and Tom Keats (Dec. 1817), *Poetry Foundation*, https://www.poetryfoundation.org/articles/69384/selections-from-keatss-letters.

Statement 48: Masha Gessen, "The Putin Paradigm," *The New York Review of Books* (Dec. 13, 2016), https://www.nybooks.com/daily/2016/12/13/putin-paradigm-how-trump-will-rule/.

Statement 50: A paraphrase of Walt Whitman's "Do I contradict myself? / Very well then I contradict myself," from *Song of Myself*. The complete text of the poem may be found at https://www.poetryfoundation.org/poems/45477/song-of-myself-1892-version.

Envoi: The Marvelous

Statement 6: Sarah Kershaw, "The Psychology of Moving," *The New York Times* (Feb. 28, 2010), https://www.nytimes.com/2010/02/28/realestate/28cov.html.

Statement 9: "What to Know About Birth Control and Blood Clots," *Cleveland Clinic* (Apr. 26, 2022), https://health.clevelandclinic.org/yes-your-birth-control-could-make-you-more-likely-to-have-a-blood-clot/. While the pill increases a woman's chance of developing clots, that increased chance is still lower than the one caused by pregnancy itself. Sigh.

Statement 11: Mark Leviton, "We Will Be Seen: Tressie McMillan Cottom on Confronting Racism, Sexism, and Classism," *The Sun* (Feb. 2020), https://www.thesunmagazine.org/issues/530/we-will-be-seen.

Statement 13: "Dada and Surrealism: Introduction," *Oxford Art Online*, https://www.oxfordartonline.com/page/dada-and-surrealism; "World War I and Dada," *MoMALearning*, https://www.moma.org/learn/moma_learning/themes/dada/.

Statement 15: "Pulmonary Embolism," *Cleveland Clinic*, https://my.clevelandclinic.org/health/diseases/17400-pulmonary-embolism.

Statement 17: Nikki Wallschlaeger (@nikkimwalls), 11:56 a.m. (Jan. 14, 2020), https://twitter.com/nikkimwalls/status/1217128373685604352.

Statement 18: Rob Haskell, "Serena Williams on Motherhood, Marriage, and Making Her Comeback," *Vogue* (Jan. 10, 2018), https://www.vogue.com/article/serena-williams-vogue-cover-interview-february-2018.

Statement 21: Charles Patrick Davis, ed. George Schiffman, "Pulmonary Embolism," *eMedicineHealth*, https://www.emedicinehealth.com/pulmonary_embolism/article_em.htm.

Statement 29: Philip Metres and Mark Nowak, "Poetry as Social Practice in the First Person Plural: A Dialogue on Documentary Poetics," *Iowa Journal of Cultural Studies*, vol. 12/13 (Spring & Fall 2010): 11, https://pubs.lib.uiowa.edu/ijcs/article/29881/galley/138224/view/.

Statement 34: David Gascoyne, *A Short Survey of Surrealism* (City Lights Books, 1982), 106.

FURTHER READING

IN MANY WAYS, this book is a history of my reading, and one of its great difficulties has been leaving things out, not because they weren't fascinating or relevant, but because they didn't fit the needs of particular essays. But if what you've read isn't marvelous—or hideous—enough for you, I encourage you to go down the rabbit hole of research. Here are some topics:

+ The medieval illuminated manuscript known as *The Very Rich Hours of the Duke of Berry*, preserved totally out of sight and known only to the public in reproductions.

+ The legend of Simonides the Poet, divinely inspired inventor of mnemonic devices.

+ The education of Mary Whiton Calkins, dream researcher and first female president of the American Psychological Association.

+ The mysterious Welsh village of Portmeirion, where the cult classic British television show about surveillance and resistance, *The Prisoner*, was filmed.

- The dream dictionary compiled through automatic writing by a nineteenth-century Chattanooga dry-goods magnate named Gustavus Hindman Miller, with entries on everything from abbots to welsh rarebit.

- Speaking of automatic writing, the story of William Butler Yeats's marriage and his subsequent development of a complex spiritual theory involving spirals and conic sections.

ACKNOWLEDGMENTS

THANKS TO the many writers and friends that read drafts of this book, including Sandra Beasley, Doritt Carroll, Joanna Penn Cooper, John Cotter, J. K. Daniels, K. Lorraine Graham, Jennifer L. Knox, Kwoya Fagin Maples, Douglas Rothschild, and Bevil Townsend. Your time, insight, and advice are greatly appreciated.

Thanks also to Michelle Chan Brown, Anselm Berrigan, Ron Slate, and Guy Pettit, who published selections from this book in *The Brooklyn Rail*, *Drunken Boat*, *On the Seawall*, and the Flying Object Pamphlet Series, as well as to Susana Gardner, through whose Dusie Press the preface was originally published as a chapbook.

My especial thanks to Elisa Gabbert, Kwoya Fagin Maples, and Natalie Shapero for their blurbs of this book.

All my gratitude to Shanna Compton, who believed in this project from the outset, and is largely responsible for the form it ultimately took—both in terms of how it went from a couple of random essays to an entire book, and then became an actual, physical book. You are a poet and publisher extraordinaire!

Finally, to Jeffrey Eaton, thanks for having a good attitude during, toward, against, through, and into our sixteen years together.

In Memoriam

Hon. Donald C. Pogue, who taught me
to think, and then think again.

1947–2016

ABOUT THE AUTHOR

MAUREEN THORSON is a poet, publisher, and book designer living in Falmouth, Maine. She is the author of the full-length collections *Share the Wealth*, published by Veliz Books in 2022, *My Resignation*, published by Shearsman Books in 2014, and *Applies to Oranges*, published in 2011 by Ugly Duckling Presse. She has also written a number of chapbooks, including *Mayport*, which won the Poetry Society of America's National Chapbook Fellowship for 2006. Her poems can be found in many anthologies and journals, including *Ploughshares*, the *Kenyon Review Online*, and *Bennington Review*. Maureen is also the founder of NaPoWriMo, an annual project in which poets attempt to write a poem a day for the month of April.